THE LANCASHIRE DERBYSHIRE AND EAST COAST RAILWAY

Chesterfield to Langwith Junction, the Beighton Branch and Sheffield District Railway

CHRIS BOOTH

FONTHILL

Fonthill Media Language Policy

Fonthill Media publishes in the international English language market. One language edition is published worldwide. As there are minor differences in spelling and presentation, especially with regard to American English and British English, a policy is necessary to define which form of English to use. The Fonthill Policy is to use the form of English native to the author. Chris Booth was born and educated in Worksop, Nottinghamshire; therefore British English has been adopted in this publication.

Fonthill Media Limited
Fonthill Media LLC
www.fonthillmedia.com
office@fonthillmedia.com

First published in the United Kingdom and the United States of America 2017

British Library Cataloguing in Publication Data:
A catalogue record for this book is available from the British Library

Typeset in 10pt on 13pt Sabon
Printed and bound by CPI Group (UK) Ltd, Croydon, CR0 4YY

Acknowledgements

I would not have been able to compile this book without the help of photographers and enthusiasts of the LD&ECR, who have allowed me access to their collections. Some of the images are well known and have been seen before; others, however, have not been published before, and are seen here for the first time. Some are nice and crisp, others not so, but are included for their rarity value. I would like to thank the following for help with photographic material: Barrie Ashton, Allan Bailey, Neil Baker, Kevin Birkinshaw, Martin Bromley, Peter Churchman, John Cole, Paul Cooke, Joe Clarke, John Gilkes, Ken Grainger, Syd Hancock, John Law, Lawson Little, Bernard Mettam, Brian Newboult, Kevin Medford, Michael Rhodes, Peter Rose, Alan Rowles, Alan Smalley, Adrian Stretton, Ivan Summers, Ian Stringer, Derek Talbot, Howard Turner, Brian Tutt, Brian Wragg, Bill Wright, Phil Whitehead, and Brian Young.

A very special thank you to Derek Talbot, Lawson Little, and Barrie Ashton for allowing me to copy their extensive collection of images and information. For help with the text of the book, I also thank Lawson Little, an acknowledged expert on all things LD&ECR, and Phil Whitehead, who supplied colliery information.

Thanks to Roger Newman and John Bennett for information regarding signalling, to John Cole and Neil Baker for timetables, and to Glynne Waite for tickets. The staff at Nottingham City Library were helpful in finding maps, and Graeme Bickerdike, editor of the Forgotten Relics website, allowed me use of information about Scarcliffe Station. Thanks to Ian Whelpton, the Sales and Marketing Director for W. H. Davis Ltd, for allowing use of the aerial shot of their works. Thanks also to the Network Rail Archives for use of diagrams. If I have forgotten anyone, I apologise, but they are thanked also.

Chris Booth
Langold
Nottinghamshire
2017

Contents

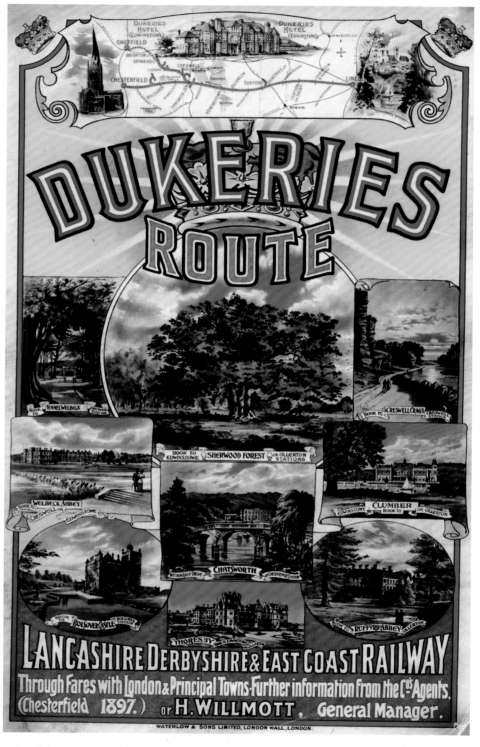

A colourful poster issued by the LD&ECR to extoll the virtues of the surrounding areas, such as Clumber Park, Bolsover Castle, Welbeck Abbey, and Sherwood Forest. (*Author's collection*)

Introduction

In the days when coal was 'king', an ambitious plan was laid by a group of coal owners, led by William Arkwright (a decendent of the inventor and entrepreneur, Richard Arkwright), for an east to west cross-country rail route connecting the Manchester Ship Canal at Warrington to a new dock that would be built near the small east coast village of Sutton-on-Sea. It was to be grandly titled the Lancashire, Derbyshire and East Coast Railway (LD&ECR). As history was to show, this line would reach neither Warrington nor Sutton-on-Sea, with only the Chesterfield to Pyewipe Junction section and a branch to Sheffield ever being completed. Taken over by the Great Central Railway (GCR) in 1907, the route was primarily a coal-carrying railway, with a passenger service that lasted until 1955. Here, you can discover the self-styled 'Dukeries Route' and its branches through the lenses of photographers from a period of over 110 years. From the main line between Chesterfield and Lincoln to the Beighton Branch, the Sheffield District Railway, and the Mansfield Railway to the motive power depots at Tuxford and Langwith Junction, this is a photographic journey from yesterday to today, bringing you the story of the railway from its early days to what remains in 2017.

I have been fascinated with this railway since stumbling across a copy of the Oakwood Press book *The Lancashire Derbyshire and East Coast Railway* by Jack Cupit and Bill Taylor, first published in 1966. It was reprinted in 1984 and 1988, but the line then featured very little in book form until Lawson Little published his book *Langwith Junction: The Life and Times of a Railway Village* in 1995. Since then, apart from the odd article in the railway press, little else has been seen in book form.

I decided to redress this balance, but I did not wish to delve too deeply into the nuts and bolts of the railway. As such, my books are but a potted history of the LD&ECR line, the Beighton Branch, and the Sheffield District Railway, along with its later connections and colliery branches. It is with the help of the individuals who have allowed me access to their photographic collections that I have been able to compile them.

Known by some as the 'East to West' and by others as the 'Dukeries Route', Volume One will explore the line from Chesterfield to Langwith Junction, then along the Beighton Branch to the Sheffield District Railway. It will also look at Chesterfield,

Tuxford, and Langwith Junction motive power depots, and a brief introduction to the original signalling of the line.

Volume Two will cover the remaining section to Pyewipe Junction, along with the Mansfield Railway connection. This end of the route was mostly intact until the 1980s, and some of it is still *in situ* today; however, since the movement of coal ceased along the line with the closure of the one remaining colliery at Thoresby, its future is uncertain.

I do hope that, in viewing these photographs and information, it leads to a further interest in the railway and that you will get a deeper understanding of the line dubbed 'The Dukeries Route'.

1

The History and the Route (including Later Branches)

The history of the LD&ECR is linked with the desire to tap the rich coalfields in the East Midlands. The plan was to construct the railway from a deep-water dock on the Manchester Ship Canal at Warrington, to new docks on the Lincolnshire coast at Sutton-on-Sea, thus allowing an outlet on either coast for the export of coal.

Before looking further, though, we have to know about the Newark and Ollerton Railway. The first proposals for a line from the Great Northern Railway (GNR) main line at South Muskham near Newark (in Nottinghamshire) via Ollerton to Worksop (also in Nottinghamshire) were suggested in 1878, but came to nothing. This would have afforded the GNR a route to Manchester, running powers permitted. The main trade of Ollerton at the time was the production of hops for the brewing trade and in 1881 a second proposal was laid before Parliament for a proposed Newark and Ollerton Railway (NOR), but again had no success. However, modified plans submitted in 1886 were authorised on 5 July 1887. Promoted by Earl Manvers and the Duke of Portland, it was hoped that the GNR would run the railway; however, they did not wish to play ball.

The Duke of Portland's papers in Nottingham Archives have references to the Ollerton–Worksop extension to the NOR. The route would have left Ollerton in a north-westerly direction and paralleled the present A616, then passed Budby village, crossed the current B6034 at Carburton and ran parallel to the east of the road. Passing Truman's Lodge in Clumber Park, it would have skirted Worksop College and passed Manton (later the site of a colliery and village), then a viaduct would have been required over a road (today the B6040), the Chesterfield Canal and River Ryton, to connect with the Manchester Sheffield and Lincolnshire Railway (MS&LR) at Rayton Lane, via a west-facing junction. There were vast reserves of coal in the concealed coalfield beneath the area, and the chance of obtaining quality coal saw the planning of collieries at Ollerton, Edwinstowe (Thoresby Colliery), Bothamsall (Bevercotes), Checker House, and Manton.

William Arkwright suggested that the NOR line should be extended through his own estate to Chesterfield, but received no support from the GNR and, as such, promoted his own line, the erstwhile LD&ECR. There were a number of lines already approved that could also be incorporated—for instance, the Macclesfield and Warrington

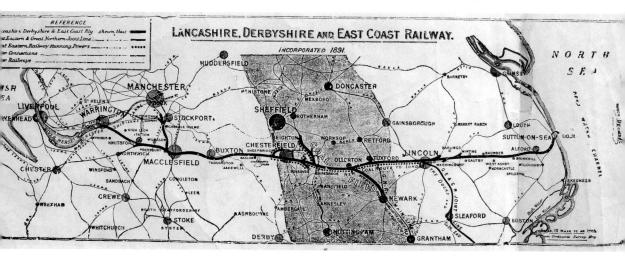

A map of the entire LD&ECR route as proposed, showing all connecting lines and routes. (*Author's collection*)

Railway and the Lincoln and East Coast Railway—that, with plans approved in 1884 for a dock at Sutton-on-Sea, would make up Arkwright's route. As the GNR were also shying away from the NOR, the promoters of the NOR approached the LD&ECR, and an agreement was signed to incorporate the NOR into the LD&ECR Act of 5 August 1891.

Incorporating the NOR would have given the LD&ECR a shorter route to London coal markets for Derbyshire coal and the planned collieries in the concealed coalfield. It would also have given the GNR access to Manchester without having to obtain running powers from the MS&LR if they were supportive of the NOR/LD&ECR line. However, the GNR passed up on this possibility.

The LD&ECR Act was opposed by the Midland Railway (MR), the MS&LR, and the London and North-Western Railway (LNWR), but the bill was passed without alteration by both Houses of Parliament. Contemporary reports stated that 'the capital of the company was £5 million with £1,666,000 borrowing powers.'

The estimated cost of the LD&ECR line was £4,227,522. Additional costs included: £200,000 for the cost of the Newark and Ollerton Railway; £100,000 to subscribe to Sutton Docks; and £15,000 for additional land at Sutton. This brought the total to £4,542,522, leaving a margin for unforeseen works and additional accommodation when the time might arise of £457,478. The construction of the line was expected to take four years, with Bolsover Tunnel being the longest work. According to other contractors, 'the work would require in the region of 10,000 men working continuously during that period.'

The NOR plans for 1881 and 1886 portray slightly different routes—the 1886 route being the same as the plans in the LD&ECR 1891 Act, while the 1881 plan shows a route to the south of the later one. In July 1892, the LD&ECR asked the GNR to help with the construction of the NOR branch, but, although they were now interested, they were not willing to subscribe £200,000 towards capital costs. Nor were they willing to share working of the branch equally in return for running powers to Chesterfield, as the LD&ECR in return wished to obtain running powers from Newark to Boston.

As the existing powers to build the branch were to expire in August 1893, Newark Town Council was approached for support in order to gain Parliamentary approval for an extension of time to construct the line. They also asked the Town Council and the GNR to contribute £40,000 each towards the cost of construction of the line, something the Town Council took exception to, as they had been told the branch would be constructed without any cost to the town. The GNR were also still reluctant to commit to the project.

By the time the LD&ECR opened for traffic in December 1896, the NOR and other extremities of the route had been abandoned, although a final try to convince the company to honour its promise to construct the NOR was made as late as December 1897. Financial considerations without help from Newark ruled this out, and the NOR was lost to obscurity.

LD&ECR Route to Chesterfield

As the line ran across the lie of the land, there were several major engineering works involved in its construction. The 170-mile-long main line of the LD&ECR was projected to run from Warrington towards the south near Wilderspool Causeway, via Knutsford, where there would be a link to the Cheshire Lines Railway. The next section would then run via the Cheshire Plain and climb through Alderley and Prestbury, with a branch from Prestbury to Cheadle Hulme, then via Cheadle and Heaton Mersey to make connections to other railways in the vicinity. It would then make a semi-circular bypass of Macclesfield, with a branch to the North Staffordshire Railway. Passing to the south of Rainow, it would then climb steeply and enter a 2.5-mile-long tunnel, where Lamaload Reservoir now exists. Continuing into the Goyt Valley, it would again enter a tunnel roughly where Errwood Reservoir is today and, after emerging, pass through the southern outskirts of Buxton.

Following a route to the south of Ashwood Vale, it would then cross Monsal Dale on a 272-foot-high steel lattice viaduct. The LD&ECR Monsal Dale Viaduct would comprise eight spans of 150 feet each, and would overshadow the MR 74-foot-high Headstone (or Monsal) Viaduct. A contemporary report in the *Derbyshire Times* read:

> The position was an exceedingly good one for building a viaduct. It would extend from hill to hill in a land locked valley, the engineer being confident that the work on this portion of the line could be carried out at the estimated cost. In fact, since the preliminary estimate was made he had got tenders for some of the work and details of all of them, with the result that in regard to the viaducts he had a margin of something close to £40,000.

From Monsal Dale, the line would drop steeply via Longstone to pass Curbar and cross the River Derwent. Climbing steeply again, it would enter a tunnel beneath the moors, and then drop steeply to Chesterfield. The estimated costs of some of the viaducts along this section of route would have been:

Macclesfield	£40,524
Deepdale	£14,000
Sandy Dale	£11,000
Monsal Dale	£73,670
Derwent	£51,595

First Sod Is Cut

The central section from Chesterfield to Pyewipe Junction near Lincoln was to be the first (and only) part to be constructed; this is now described as far as Langwith Junction.

The ceremonial cutting of the first sod of the new railway at Maynards Meadow, the site of the new station in Chesterfield, was performed by Agnes Mary Arkwright, the wife of chairman William Arkwright on 7 June 1892. She used an ebony barrow with silver mountings along with an inscribed spade to perform the ceremony to much applause, after which she gave a speech to the throngs watching the event. The event was followed by a banquet for 300 guests, held in the Stephenson Memorial Hall.

The contract for the construction of the line between Chesterfield and Warsop was to be handled by Messrs S. Pearson and Son, from Warsop to Tuxford by Messrs Baldry and Yarburgh, with the final section from Tuxford to Pyewipe Junction by Messrs Price and Wills. The contractors for the first section of the Beighton Branch from Langwith Junction to Barlborough Colliery Junction was also Messrs S. Pearson and Son, who received their contract in the autumn of 1892. The first part of the Beighton Branch opened for goods and coal trains on 16 November 1896, along with the line from Langwith to Pyewipe Junction and the colliery branches at Barlborough, Creswell, Langwith, and Warsop. Passenger traffic to Clowne began on 8 March 1897. Despite the optimism of the speeches given at the luncheon after the first sod had been cut, shareholders had been reluctant to invest in the 'East to West', as it initially was known, and, in 1894, the railway's directors had been compelled to accept an offer of support from the Great Eastern Railway (GER), with important conditions attached.

The GER hoped for a stream of coal trains from the new line, via a connection at Pyewipe Junction near Lincoln, up the Great Northern and Great Eastern Joint line (GN&GEJ) from Lincoln to March in Cambridgeshire, and on to London via Cambridge, and so they were not at all interested in providing direct access from the coalfields to the ports. The price of the GER assistance was the granting of running powers, the abandonment of plans to extend west of Chesterfield and that the section east of Lincoln should be a separate concern from the central section. The western section would be formally abandoned by an Act of 6 July 1895 and, although a new company, the Lincoln and East Coast Railway and Dock, was incorporated on 6 August 1897 to construct the eastern section, this never came to fruition and was abandoned in 1902.

There were also proposals in 1896 to build a branch to serve the Clay Cross Coal and Iron Company colliery, which would have left the main line shortly after leaving Chesterfield station, but again nothing came of this.

Chesterfield Market Place

The grand looking Chesterfield Station, fronting onto West Bars, was the headquarters of the company; the suffix 'Market Place' was later added by the GCR. The station possessed four platforms on two islands—one and two, and four and five. In the centre, in place of the missing platform three was a release line for the locomotives. It was one of only three stations along the route to have refreshment facilities, the other two being Langwith Junction and Edwinstowe.

Work on the construction of the railway in Chesterfield resulted in the re-alignment of the River Hipper and the closure of the original access to Queen's Park. As a result, the company had to pay for a new road from New Square to the Queen's Park, and for a new entrance to the Park. The result was a more prestigious access to the Park; the alternative would have been through the then insalubrious area of Wheeldon.

According to the General Purposes Sub-Committee of the Council, dated 10 July 1896, in addition to paying for the new Park Road to its junction with Wheeldon Lane, the Company had to widen the original Wheeldon Lane (renamed Park Road) from that junction along the side of the park. They also had to widen West Bars to a uniform width throughout, from New Square to the Easterly side of the cottages belonging to Mr Maynard at the Western end of West Bars. For that purpose, they had to acquire the 'Bird in Hand' and 'White Horse' Inns and 'intervening property'; the site was sold to William Stones Ltd, who built the Portland Hotel there.

In addition, the company had to pay the Corporation £200 in place of purchasing Mr Maynard's cottages so that the Corporation could purchase the cottages when the opportunity arose for widening that end of West Bars. They had to pay the Corporation £500 in discharge of the Company's liability in respect of the cost of taking down, moving and re-erecting the caretaker's house. This referred to North Lodge. In the end, the Council decided to repair it and build a new park keeper's house. The balance was to be settled by 1 November 1896, according to www.chesterfieldforum.net.

There was a large goods warehouse built at right angles to the station, a single-road carriage shed, coal wharf, timber yard, extensive siding facilities, a turntable, and a small loco shed, which will be described later.

An Edwardian scene at Chesterfield station with a group of youngsters looking at the camera, and a member of staff outside the entrance door. Opened in March 1897, the station was the headquarters of the company. Below the clock, a sign proclaims Lancashire Derbyshire and East Coast Railway 'The Dukeries Route', and beneath the canopies there are billboards advertising excursions to Cleethorpes and Skegness. The station became known as Market Place after the GCR takeover to differentiate it from the GCR station in Chesterfield, which became Central. It was closed by BR on 3 December 1951 along with the line to Langwith Junction due to the condition of Bolsover Tunnel. (*Nadin's series postcard/Author's collection*)

A view inside Market Place station at 12.10 p.m. one day in 1928, looking at the concourse. Notice the enamel 'LUX' and 'COMPO' advertisement signs among others. (*Author's collection*)

A view down West Bars in the 1950s after closure of the station: the canopies have been removed from the station, and the goods warehouse can be seen towards the top right. Above the platforms of the closed station is what is termed a 'carriage shed' on the maps, but it looks to be more of an open-sided store by this time. (*Author's collection*)

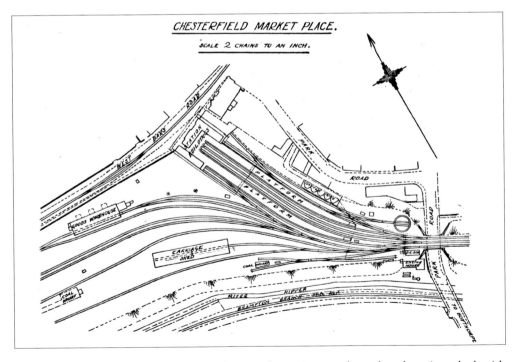

A map of the Market Place station area showing the station, goods yard, and carriage shed, with Park Road to the right. Notice the Midland Railway Brampton branch at the bottom. (*Courtesy of Network Rail corporate archive*)

Market Place Station goods yard during the First World War. Here we see two female members of staff sawing tree trunks in the goods yard, with a view towards the station from a rarely seen angle. This must be one of the earliest pictures of women in men's overalls instead of the long skirts and hats, but they are still wearing heeled shoes. (*Brian Tutt Collection*)

Stationmaster

Mr C. E. Peachey was the stationmaster at Chesterfield Market Place Station from 1901 until 1928. In March 1927, the *Derbyshire Times* reported on Mr Peachey's departure after twenty-seven years as stationmaster at Chesterfield Market Place station; interestingly, he comments that, even by 1927, passenger traffic had been affected by competition from trams and buses.

The full text of the *Derbyshire Times* report reads:

> Mr C. E. Peachey, who has been station-master at the Market Place Station (L. N. & E.), Chesterfield, for the past 27 years, has been promoted to a similar position at Ware, Hertfordshire, and will be succeeded at Market Place by Mr J. Eato, who comes from New Basford. Mr Peachey was appointed stationmaster of the Market Place station in 1900, having previously held a similar position at Edwinstowe for two years, and prior to that he was for 18 months stationmaster at Doddington and Harby.
>
> Before joining the old LD&ECR Company as a relief stationmaster, Mr Peachey was chief inspector on the City and South London Electric Railway. He came to Chesterfield Market Place station in 1896 in the mineral department, and four years later was appointed stationmaster. 'My first impression of the town', said Mr Peachey to the *Derbyshire Times* representative, 'with its narrow streets and dirty

Mr C. E. Peachey was the stationmaster at Chesterfield Market Place station from 1901 until 1928. This image shows Mr Peachey (third from the right) seeing off a train from Market Place in Great Central days. The locomotive is LD&ECR class 'C' 0-4-4T No. 13, by now GCR 1169. *(Brian Tutt Collection)*

The Chesterfield Market Place station staff, believed to be in 1916–17. In the centre is Mr C. E. Peachey, the stationmaster. The two women flanking him are his daughters Muriel (Madge) Peachey and Constance (Connie) Peachey, both of whom joined the ticket office in 1917 as conscription began to take away non-essential railway staff. Both married railwaymen who they met at Market Place station; they ended up living in Shirebrook. *(Brian Tutt Collection)*

Above: A further image of the staff from Chesterfield Market Place, with what looks like the goods depot gates behind. This seems to date from *c.* 1920–22, and Muriel and Constance Peachey are in the centre with an unknown child. The 1939 staff returns for Chesterfield Central station showed the stationmaster as John George Peabody, who was also in charge of Chesterfield Market Place. Also employed at Market Place station were the following staff:

Porters: Arthur Wingfield and Leslie Arthur Pearson.
Working Foreman: John Bennet.
Goods Porters: Henry Collins, William Ellis, and Arthur Buxton.
Shunters: Sydney George Barwick and Harold George Turner.
Carriage Cleaner: Lionel Schofield.

Perhaps some of these men are in the photos. (*Brian Tutt Collection*)

Below: The earliest of the group shots from Market Place in Great Central days, and possibly from before the First World War. Mr C. E. Peachey is in the middle of quite a large group of all-male staff (the First World War saw the employment of women in significant numbers, as other photos show). The poster to the left advertises Whitsuntide specials to Lincoln, Cleethorpes and Grimsby. Notice the awkward sitting position of the young lad in front. (*Brian Tutt Collection*)

Former LD&ECR class 'C' 0-4-4T tank No. 17, by now GCR 1151B, at Chesterfield Market Place, date unknown (but between 1907–1923). Six of these locomotives were designed for the LD&ECR by Kitsons of Leeds, and were built between 1897 and 1898. Later LNER Class G3, they were unique as the only true passenger type owned by the LD&ECR. They were used on the LD&ECR's main line between Lincoln and Chesterfield, but also worked into the Sheffield (Midland) station. During GCR ownership, many of this class carried duplicate numbers with suffix 'B' or 'C' letters. All were eventually renumbered with unique numbers during the LNER renumbering scheme of 1924, with this one becoming 6403. During the 1920s, five of the class would end up restricted to the Sheffield Area. The sixth (No. 6404) was moved to the West Riding and worked out of Ardsley, and would be the first to be withdrawn in 1931. The other five engines were withdrawn between 1931 and 1935, this one in March 1933. (*Brian Tutt collection*)

conditions was anything but satisfactory. There were no buses or electric trams, only the old horse drawn trams, and as a consequence the traffic at this station was very much heavier than it is today. But during these long years, a wonderful improvement has taken place, and I have grown to love the place as much as a native, and am extremely sorry that I am leaving'.

During the time Mr Peachey has been in Chesterfield he has been prominently identified with the Congregational Church. On coming to the town, he became associated with the Soresby Street Church, and later, when he went to live in New Hall Road, he attended the Brampton Congregational Church, and has for the last eight years taken the Young Men's Class.

To make the esteem and affection in which he was held by the staff at the Market Place Station, Mr. Peachey was on Saturday morning made the recipient of an umbrella bearing the description 'From the staff and friends, Chesterfield M.P. Station, March 1927' and a wallet, and Mrs. Peachey received a handbag. The presentation ceremony, which took place in Mr. Peachey's office, in the presence of the whole staff, was made by signalman J. Grennon, the oldest member, who expressed in suitable words the regret they all felt at the departure of Mr. Peachey. He spoke of the happy relationship which had always existed between Mr Peachey and the staff, and said that while they were sorry to lose him, they were pleased to hear of his promotion, and wished both him and Mrs Peachey the best of good luck in their new sphere.

Mr T. Clarke, who was formerly on the clerical staff, said that Mr Peachey would be in the same office as he (the speaker) had worked in at the age of twelve years, when his father was station-master there. Mr C. Hyde and Mr J. F. Beaumont also spoke in eulogistic terms of Mr. Peachey's long service at the Market Place Station.

Mr Peachey, in acknowledging the gifts and the kind expressions, recalled that signalman Grennon and Mr Kilby were then members of the staff, and had had nearly twenty-seven years under his control. 'During the whole time I have been here,' said Mr Peachey, 'the most pleasant co-operation and good feeling has always existed between myself and the staff, and I can only hope that in my new sphere I shall have the same loyal feeling and co-operation as I have had here'.

Mrs. Peachey, in a happy little speech, thanked the staff for the handsome present she had received. 'I shall go away with a sad heart' she said, 'because I had hoped that we would finish our days here, and I tell Mr Peachey that I am looking forward to two years' time when we can come back and retire here'.

It is now early nationalisation and Robinson A5 4-6-2T 69818 waits to depart from the station with a train for Lincoln. This loco was GCR 374. Introduced to service on 30 September 1917, it became LNER 5374, then 9818, before receiving its BR number. It would be withdrawn on 31 December 1958 from 38B Annesley shed and would end its days at Darlington scrapyard in February 1959. (*Author's collection*)

Robinson J11 0-6-0 64321 waits to depart from Market Place station in 1951. Introduced to service on 31 October 1902, it was allocated to 40E Langwith Junction at the time of the photo, being withdrawn from 36E Retford on 20 July 1959. It was disposed of at Gorton Works in September 1959. (*Author's collection*)

An unidentified K3 2-6-0 approaches Chesterfield Market Place station in 1949. On the right is the Saxby and Farmer signal box built to a design unique to this railway. Opened in March 1897, it had a Saxby and Farmer eighty-lever frame. Although there is no date for closure of the box, it is derelict in photos taken in 1956 so it was before goods services ceased in 1957. Beyond the box is the home signal: this had a four-way route indicator and was worked by levers seventy-one, seventy-two, seventy-three, or seventy-five, depending on which route was selected. In October 1939, the staff returns showed that two class five signalmen were employed in the signal box—Frank Gooding, who entered service on 6 December 1926, and James Charles Long, who entered service on 9 July 1934. (*Author's collection*)

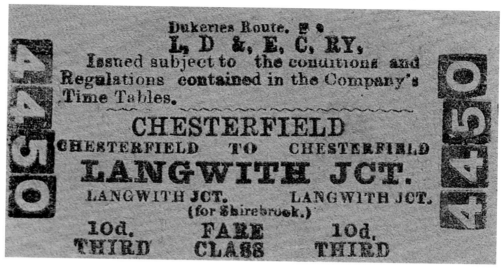

Like other railway companies, the LD&ECR issued Edmondson card tickets to travellers for the destinations along the route, and quite a few of these survive today. Glynne Waite has a great collection of these and has kindly allowed a selection to be shown in the book. Here are examples of tickets from the LD&ECR annotated Chesterfield and LNER with the subtitle Market Place, as it was called by the GCR. (*Glynne Waite collection*)

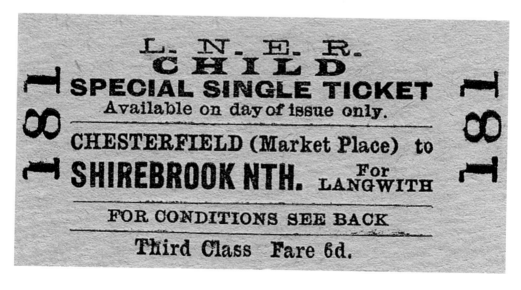

Stephenson Exhibition

Over four days in August 1948, a railway exhibition was held at Market Place to celebrate the centenary of the death of George Stephenson. Opened to the public on Thursday 12 August at 10.30 a.m., the official opening was performed by the mayor, Alderman Edgar Smith, at 6.45 p.m., with the Sunday opening by the 'Railway Queen', Miss Janet Taylor from Leeds, at 10.30 a.m. Admission was 6*d* for adults and 3*d* for children, with a programme costing an additional 2*d*. Some 30,000 people were expected to attend; the actual figure was 38,221, including almost 13,000 children. Around £900 was raised from admission and programme sales and, after costs were deducted, the profits were destined for 'selected funds and charities.'

Contemporary newspaper reports stated that 1,000 people visited in the first hour alone, with a 100-yard queue on the street outside by early afternoon. On Sunday, the final day, a 230-yard queue had formed for the opening by the Railway Queen, who was met by Mr A. H. Peppercorn, the Chief Mechanical Engineer of the Eastern and North-Eastern Regions of British Railways.

Historical exhibits mentioned in the commemorative brochure were a full-scale replica of Rocket, Liverpool and Manchester Railway 1838-built 0-4-0 *Lion*, Midland Railway 4-2-2 'single' locomotive No. 118, and a Great Central Railway 'Director' D10 Class, 62658 *Prince George*. Historical coaching exhibits included Queen Victoria's LNWR saloon, London and Birmingham Railway Queen Adelaide's saloon and the LNER's 'Coronation beaver-tail' observation coach, along with 'signalling instruction and exhibition vans.'

Modern locomotives were an ex-LMS 'Patriot' class No. 45529, which was named *Stephenson* at the event, and an ex-LNER class 61085. Two parcel vans contained small exhibits with large-scale locomotive models, a model of an early Liverpool and Manchester Railway passenger coach, old photographs, engravings, and historical documents 'many signed by George Stephenson', along with some items from the York Railway Museum. A small signalling exhibition was inside a van, with items on display including an electric point motor, block instruments, relays and the like. There was also a display of rolling stock, which included a 1947 Doncaster Works-built coach, a new Wolverton-built corridor coach, and a buffet lounge car from the 'Flying Scotsman' coaching set. Wagons on display included a 16-ton steel-bodied mineral wagon—part of a batch of 1,000 then being built by the Derbyshire Carriage and Wagon Co. Ltd at New Whittington—and a milk wagon.

According to Lawson Little, a well-known LD&ECR aficionado, platforms one and two were used to house the rolling stock display, and those not paying were denied a free look by a set of coaches parked in the centre road in the station area, while platforms four and five were used for service trains.

The May 1954 *Trains Illustrated* magazine supports an article entitled 'The Junctions at Shirebrook' by Roger Brettle:

The connections at Shirebrook Junction (taken out in 1951) enabled a special from Crewe with London Midland Region stock to be brought to the exhibition The

Market Place was the obvious choice for the site of an exhibition to celebrate the centenary of the death of George Stephenson. The exhibition occupied much of the two platforms nearest to the goods yard, the latter also being largely given over to the occasion. The station would probably never had hosted such large crowds since its opening days. There was a strong LMS presence, which included the Liverpool and Manchester Railway *Lion*, a MR Class 156 2-4-0 No. 158A and here Midland Railway's 'Spinner' 4-2-2 No. 118 is the background to a family photo. (*Brian K Young collection*)

B1 61085 and former GCR D10 62658 *Prince George*, both fresh out of the paint shop, head a line up on the goods yard approach lines. (*Author's collection*)

train arrived at Shirebrook (West) headed by the newly rebuilt 'Patriot' No. 45529, its freshly fitted Stephenson nameplates covered by wood, and hauling, amongst an assorted load, the Johnson single M.R. No. 118, the M.R. 2-4-0 No. 158A (later L.M.S. No. 20002), LNWR No. 3020 Cornwall, LNWR No. 790 Hardwicke, a replica of Rocket, with tender, and Lion. However, someone had blundered, so it was decided that Cornwall and Hardwicke were unwanted guests; they were removed and spent the period of the Exhibition in a coal siding at Mansfield shed. Langwith 'B1' No. 61085 was substituted for the 'Patriot' and the remainder of this remarkable cavalcade then pounded up the gradient to Langwith Junction on its way to Chesterfield.

Sadly this was the swan song of the Market Place Station as just three years later passenger services were withdrawn due to the condition of Bolsover Tunnel and the station closed. With the withdrawal of goods facilities in March 1957, trackwork was lifted and the station buildings taken over by Charles Credland Ltd paint manufacturer.

Robinson J11 0-6-0 64336 at Chesterfield Market Place on 4 March 1957. This was apparently the final loco moved to the station, and its job was to clear all remaining wagons from the goods yard. Note the cattle dock to the right with the Portland Hotel beyond. The platform three starting signal is off; however, the footplate of the loco is deserted—maybe the photographer, who is standing on the signal bracket in the above photo, is one of the crew. The loco was built by Beyer Peacock Ltd and entered service on 31 October 1903. Allocated to 38D Staveley, it was withdrawn on 13 July 1959 and disposed of at Gorton Works later that month. (*Ken Grainger collection*)

The station after closure was used by paint manufacturers Charles Credland Ltd, whose vans can be seen on the former concourse. Now devoid of canopies, the platforms are growing weeds and the air of dereliction pervades. (*Author's collection*)

Onwards to Langwith

After leaving Market Place Station, the line immediately crossed Park Road on Bridge No. 1, a brick-arched bridge with a span of 40 foot and a height of 20 foot above the road. The line then crossed the River Hipper, followed by the two spans and two arches of Boythorpe Viaduct, which carried the main line over the MR Brampton Branch and the industrial Boythorpe Railway. Here there was also a steeply graded zigzag line down into the Bryan Donkin Company sidings.

After this, the line continued on a high embankment and crossed the eleven spans of the Horns Bridge viaduct, which took it 63 feet above the A61 and A617 roads, the MR main line, the GCR Chesterfield Loop line and the River Rother. This had seven brick arches, four lattice deck girders and a bowstring bridge. The company had emblazoned the viaduct with its logo 'The Dukeries Route', as the LD&ECR styled itself as it was being built through, and close to, the lands of several of the North Nottinghamshire Dukes. This section of line was a deviation of the original route passed by the Act of Parliament of 1891. More information about this and other deviations to the original plans, can be found in the excellent book *Tracing the Lancashire Derbyshire and East Coast Railway* by Zoe Elizabeth Hunter.

Above: A different view of the signal box taken from Park Road looking towards town; Market Place station would be to the left. The image has no date, but it was possibly taken *c.* 1940s or 1950s. The gates on the right are for the level crossing on the Midland Railway's Brampton branch, which crossed the road at this point. Notice the large signal gantry devoid of any signal arms, so this might signify their recent replacement. Clearly the old gantry had at least five arms: the left (lower) reading to the goods yard, while the other four into their respective platforms—this was perhaps replaced by a single post with a four-way route indicator. (*Terry Harry Young collection*)

Below: Not the best image, but this shows Boythorpe Viaduct, which was between Market Place station and Horns Bridge. It is seen here with a J11 crossing on a freight. The viaduct crossed the MR Brampton branch and the Boythorpe Colliery branch. The wagons in the foreground are in the sidings for the Lincoln and Universal works, of Bryan Donkin Co. Ltd, Derby Road, Chesterfield. The company was founded 1803 by Bryan Donkin, an engineer and inventor. In 1900, it was merged with Clench & Co. Ltd of Chesterfield and relocated to the works at Derby Road, Chesterfield from Bermondsey. In 1931, the works covered 14 acres. In this image, their internal steam loco is in the process of shunting. The LD&EC access to this yard was via a zigzag, which dropped down to the right of the viaduct. Bryan Donkin closed in 1999 and the site is now residential homes, with the crooked spire of St Mary and All Saints dominating the skyline. (*Neil Baker collection*)

Horns Bridge viaduct carried the Dukeries Route of the LD&ECR into Chesterfield from Spital. It spanned Derby Road, Hasland Road, the Midland and Great Central Railway (Chesterfield loop), and the River Rother. The line continued to the west on a high embankment, before terminating at Market Place station. Demolition began in 1960, with the last section being removed in 1985 to allow for alterations to Derby Road and the building of Horns Bridge roundabout. Today, a small section of the viaduct can still be seen between Frankie & Benny's restaurant and the existing Horns Bridge at the bottom of Hasland Road. This photo was in *Engineering Magazine* on 15 December 1899. (*Author's collection*)

The famous view of Chesterfield's three railways. It shows the GCR Chesterfield Loop at the bottom, with the Midland Railway across the centre. A coal train is just making its way north with at least three Shirebrook Colliery private owner wagons in the consist. To the right of the picture is Horns Bridge signal box, with a set of tall MR lower quadrant signals in front. Across the top of the photo a LD&ECR train, headed by what looks like a class 'C' 0-4-4T, steams off towards Bolsover, the brick arch it is crossing being emblazoned with 'Dukeries Route'. (*Neil Baker collection*)

Another view of the three railways, this time in the 1960s. An unidentified 9F 2-10-0 is making its way along the Midland line, and as can be seen, the Dukeries Route is no more as the bridge girders have been removed. On the Midland line, Horns Bridge signal box can be observed on the right of the image, but it is not much longer for this world, as its replacement is being built just below the signals. This new box opened in May 1963, but the construction seems to have just started; with the amount of work involved, it is suggested that the date is autumn 1962. (*Derek Talbot collection*)

Another view of the viaduct shows the footbridge across the GCR line, with MR line in the centre of the image and the LD&ECR at the top. The footbridge was a popular spot to watch trains as all three routes could be observed: it was known as 'the Forty Steps'. (*Author's collection*)

A higher view of Horns Bridge viaduct in the 1950s sees a train on the Midland line just disappearing off right centre of photo. Just below the first arch, on the left of the photo, is the buffer stop for the first part of the zigzag down to the Bryan Donkin works. (*Neil Baker collection*)

Viewed from road level on Lordsmill Street, there are no vehicles, just a window cleaner with his cart and a few onlookers. The only part of the viaduct that remains today is a small section of the pier to the left of the window cleaner. (*Author's collection*)

After passing over the viaducts and heading towards Langwith, we come to Dingle Bank. Here we see a train passing Dingle Bank on the way into Chesterfield; the image is taken from Hady Lane Bridge, looking towards Dingle Lane Bridge, which the train is just passing over. The bridge in the background is No. 8, a three-span farmer's occupation bridge. Today, although the embankment remains, the cutting beyond the train is filled in and the houses to the right on Dingle Bank have gone. The train looks like it is headed by a C12 4-4-2T with five six-wheel coaches. (*Roy Riggott collection*)

The route then continued through Spital, passing over the small arched Bridge No. 4 that crossed Spital Lane with an embankment on top of it. It then continued through cuttings and embankments and passed under Hady Lane (Bridge No. 6) then passed Lower Hady, before passing over Bridge No. 7 at Dingle Bank, where once there were around twelve houses and a shop.

Calow and Bonds Main Branch

Still heading east and now uphill at 1-in-100, there was an aqueduct across the line to feed farmers' fields. This consisted of a steel trough that was 4 foot and 7 inches wide at a height of 25 foot above the railway, after which came Bridge No. 10 beneath Dark Lane. Beyond this was the Calow and Bonds Main Branch, which headed off southward, down to the collieries of the same name.

Work on a new colliery at Grassmoor began in 1861, and the MR opened a branch from Avenue Sidings to serve it in 1872. With the opening of the MS&LR Chesterfield Loop line through Grassmoor in 1893, there was a further connection laid and, with the sinking of Bonds Main colliery in 1897, the MS&LR opened a connection to that colliery on 13 May 1901.

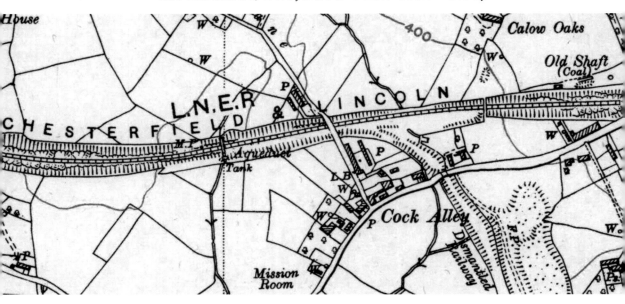

A map of the former junction area at Calow. Chesterfield is to the left and Arkwright to the right, the bridge crossing the line in the centre is Dark Lane, Bridge No. 10. The Calow and Bonds Main branch line is shown as a dismantled railway on this map, which is dated 1914. (*Author's collection*)

The site of Calow Junction on 13 October 1952, looking west from Dark Lane towards Chesterfield. There were a couple of sidings for the Calow branch here; the signal box would have been the other side of the bridge behind the camera. (*Ken Boulter/Author's collection*)

The LD&ECR had built platforms at Calow Junction, but not for public use. However, the company was casting around for traffic to serve them and looked at serving the Grassmoor and Bonds Main collieries. Plans were put forward for a branch from Calow, and parliamentary approval was gained in 1897 for the Temple Normanton and Grassmoor Branch. Not long after, the Staveley Coal and Iron Co, owners of Bonds Main, announced that they would be sinking a pit, which became Calow Main colliery. As such, the LD&ECR planned a branch to that colliery and, in the process, abandoned parts of the Temple Normanton Branch.

In the meantime, the MR had received approval for their branch to Bonds Main colliery, known as the New Grassmoor Branch. This would have joined the LD&ECR Temple Normanton and Grassmoor Branch very close to the colliery, in effect giving three points of access to Bonds Main and Grassmoor collieries. Fortunately sanity prevailed, and an agreement of 21 December 1899 saw a joint railway planned instead: this became the Calow and Bonds Main Joint Railway, with the LD&ECR, MR, and MS&LR as joint partners.

The new LD&ECR Branch was 1.5 miles long but very steep, as it served Calow and then dropped down into the valley of the Calow Brook, around 100 feet lower, at a gradient of 1-in-50/54, before going up a steep grade into Bonds Main Colliery sidings. Mitchell Brothers of Glasgow won the contract to build the branch at a cost of £12,386, which was equally divided between the three companies.

The first section to be built was the 600-metre-long single line from Calow Junction to Calow Main, which opened in November 1899. The Joint line to Bonds Main commenced operations from 6 May 1901, the LD&ECR being first users, followed by the GCR, although there is some doubt as to whether the GCR worked to Calow. The MR opened their branch from Grassmoor Junction to Bonds Main North Junction on 9 June 1901; this included a 110-yard-long Mansfield Road tunnel beneath the road and the GCR Chesterfield Loop line. Two through running sidings were built, capable of holding forty wagons each, alongside the Joint line between Bonds Main North Junction and Bonds Main Colliery.

On the LD&ECR, the cutting at Bridge 10, Dark Lane, was widened to allow for the construction of a Down Goods Loop, but, as the bridge itself had two side spans of 26 foot and a central span of 27 foot, there was no requirement to change it. The material removed from the cutting side was used to create land in the 'V' of the junction for three sidings. A new Calow Junction signal box was provided to work the sidings and junction, this having a thirty-two-lever frame.

The MR provided a signal box at Bonds Main Colliery North Junction, which controlled the entrance to the through sidings at the Calow end, and the GCR Bonds Main Colliery Sidings box controlled the other entrance. The joint line was controlled by Electric Train Tablet, the tablet sections being Calow Colliery (LD&ECR) to Bonds Main North Junction (MR) and Bonds Main Colliery Sidings (GCR), with the Up direction being designated from Calow to Bonds Main Colliery.

From 2 September 1901, the MR allowed the LD&ECR to run trains between Bonds Main and Grassmoor Junction over their new Grassmoor Railway. The MR itself worked this LD&ECR traffic from Grassmoor Junction, where a reversal was

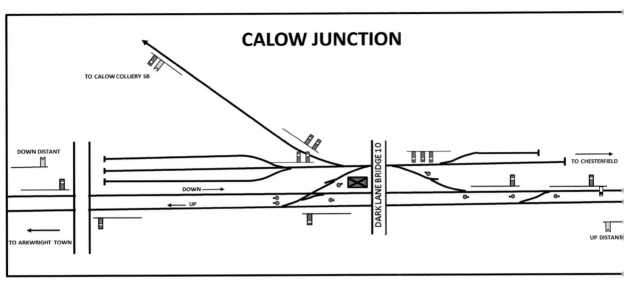

CALOW JUNCTION

TO CALOW COLLIERY SB

DOWN DISTANT

TO ARKWRIGHT TOWN

DOWN →

← UP

DARK LANE BRIDGE 10

TO CHESTERFIELD

UP DISTANT

A representation of the signal box diagram from Calow Junction, taken from a hand-drawn plan found in the National Archives at Kew by John Bennett. On this diagram, Arkwright is to the left with Chesterfield to the right. It is thought that, once closed, the signal box was re-used at Clipstone East Junction. (*Author's collection*)

Looking east at Calow Junction on 4 September 1955 from Dark Lane Bridge. Calow Junction signal box would have been on the right of the image, possibly where the large bush is. The trackbed for the Calow Branch can be seen as it sweeps off towards the top right corner. (*Ken Boulter/Author's collection*)

Robinson 9J (later J11) 0-6-0 1000 is seen at Grassmoor and Bond's Main Colliery signal box on the GCR Chesterfield Loop Line in an undated shot from before 1908. The loco looks almost new—as it was introduced to service on 30 April 1902, it could suggest the date is sometime in 1902. On grouping, GCR locos had 5000 added to their number: the GCR number 1000 would become LNER number 6000 until the 1944–46 renumberings, when it became 4307, and, later under BR, 64307. The loco behind it looks like either a MS&LR Sacre or Parker 0-6-0. The signal box is a typical GCR installation; the bracket signals behind the box are for the routes towards Bond's Main North Junction where the LD&ECR and Midland connections from the colliery diverged. The signal is reading to at least three routes, and it once read to four, all off a running line behind the box—notice the redundant doll on the bracket. (*Derek Talbot collection*)

necessary to run to and from Grassmoor Colliery. For this privilege, the MR charged the LD&ECR 4*d* a ton.

The severe gradient at the north end of the joint line made it difficult to operate and, when the GCR took over the LD&ECR in 1907, the requirement for it ceased, as the GCR had their own direct access to Bonds Main and Grassmoor collieries off the Chesterfield Loop. As such, the MR Bonds Main North Junction box closed on 15 November 1909, with the LD&ECR section of the joint line following on 17 November. Ground frames were installed to allow access and egress to the two running sidings that were in use. These sidings were abolished from 7 March 1910, one being lifted and the other converted to a dead-end siding with access from the former Bonds Main Junction end.

Calow and Arkwright Collieries

The history of Calow Main and Arkwright Collieries is closely linked, as both were drift mines established approximately 2.5 miles east of Chesterfield. A drift mine accesses the coal seams via inclined, sloping tunnels, as opposed to vertical shafts—also referred to as 'adit' or 'footrill' mines.

Early small-scale coal workings in this area had predominantly accessed the Blackshale and Yard seams, where they outcropped from the Brimington Anticline. This geological feature created outcrops of the coal seams on both sides of a long ridge, running from Brimington down towards Calow and beyond. This aided coal extraction by providing easy, shallow and relatively horizontal access to the seam at the edges of the ridge. As the edges of the seams were worked out, more sophisticated technological solutions to continue exploiting the seams were required. Coal seams to the west of the anticline tended to be shallower, to the east the seams were much thicker and deeper, and so led to the migration of the coalfield eastwards as technology, ventilation and the markets for coal all increased—later collieries such as Bolsover and Markham are examples of this expansion of the coalfield in an easterly direction.

Calow Main was the first large-scale deep mine in this locality, reported as working in 1863 under several owners until taken over by the Staveley Coal and Iron Company (Staveley Co.) in 1897. The Staveley Co. extended the existing two drifts down to the Top Hard seam in 1897–98 and, in January 1908, an underground connection was made with the nearby Bonds Main Colliery. Calow initially worked the Blackshale and Top Hard seam and also the Deep Soft seam by the 1920s. Production ceased in 1934; however, it was not sealed off but became an integral component of Arkwright Colliery.

As for Bonds Main Colliery, in 1882 the Staveley Co. was unable to meet demand for its coal from its current group of collieries and leased 5,000 acres of coal reserves on the Sutton estates from William Arkwright. Sinking commenced in 1895 and, in keeping with the Staveley Co., the colliery was named after one of its principal directors, George Bond. The shafts initially reached a depth of 403 feet, with an initial estimated output of 2,000 tons per week. Shafts later reached 250 yards to the Deep Hard and 373 yards to the Blackshale seam. Closed in 1921 and put up for sale by the Staveley Co., it was purchased and re-opened by the Clay Cross Co. Ltd in 1923–1924. New seams were opened up, and output in 1948 was just short of 100,000 tons from the Tupton seam. However, the colliery was abandoned on 28 May 1949.

Duckmanton Tunnel and Arkwright Town Station

Shortly after the Calow Branch the line climbed at 1-in-100 as far as the first summit within the 501-yard Duckmanton Tunnel, the eastern portion being on a falling gradient of 1-in-100. The tunnel took the line beneath Bolehill, and the village of Duckmanton was 2 miles to the north-east. The tunnel was built straight and passed through several coal seams, being 200 yards from the surface at its deepest. It was built with masonry parapets, and both its lining and portals were constructed with blue engineering brick. Water was a problem while building: construction was halted for six weeks at one point due to an inrush of water from old mine workings.

After exiting the tunnel, the line went beneath Deepsick Lane through Bridge No. 12, a three-arch bridge, and then Bridge No. 13, beneath the GCR Sheffield to London main line, and then beneath Bridge No. 14, which took the railway beneath Sutton Lane and into the first station at Arkwright Town. Originally to have been called Duckmanton, this station was renamed Arkwright Town shortly before it opened, allegedly at the request of the Staveley Company.

The 501-yard-long Duckmanton Tunnel's west end portal. The tunnel was opened in March 1897 but, when the line from Chesterfield Market Place to Langwith Junction was closed in 1951, the line through the tunnel to Arkwright Town was singled. This section remained open to goods traffic until March 1957, after which the tunnel became redundant. During the 1970s, track through the tunnel was lifted and the tunnel was filled with colliery waste from Arkwright Colliery. The tunnel's eastern approach cutting remained in use by trains serving Arkwright Colliery, which ran into the cutting to reverse into the colliery and vice versa. The eastern entrance cutting is still visible and accessible, just off the A632 Chesterfield to Bolsover road on Deepsick Lane, where the bridge over the line still remains. The western end of the tunnel and cutting has been completely hidden by land fill. Notice the colour light signal guarding the tunnel entrance. (*D. Ibbotson/Author's collection*)

Above: At the other end of Duckmanton Tunnel was Arkwright Town station. This Nadin's Series postcard dated 1906 shows some of the station staff. Prior to the railway, few buildings existed in this area, which was known as Duckmanton Moor; the original intention of the LD&ECR was to name their station 'Duckmanton'. It was only at the request of the Staveley Company that the name was changed to Arkwright Town. This view is looking towards Lincoln, with Arkwright Station signal box at the far end of the platforms. This box opened with the line in September 1898 but, when the Duckmanton curves were built in 1907, it was superseded by Arkwright Town Junction box, about 0.25 miles towards Bolsover on 13 March that year. (*Author's collection*)

Opposite: Arkwright Town was originally to have been named Duckmanton, but was renamed Arkwright Town shortly before it opened. However, by this time the tickets had been printed with the name Duckmanton and, in most cases, these were actually used until stocks ran out, after which they were printed with the new name of Arkwright Town. The exception was that tickets to destinations off the LD&ECR system had to be reprinted with the new name to enable the Railway Clearing House to properly apportion revenue. However, in this case, they used the hybrid name of Arkwright Town (Duckmanton). Eventually, the new name of Arkwright Town began to appear on all tickets: these three tickets show the variations, Duckmanton, Arkwright Town (Duckmanton), and finally Arkwright Town. (*Glynne Waite collection*)

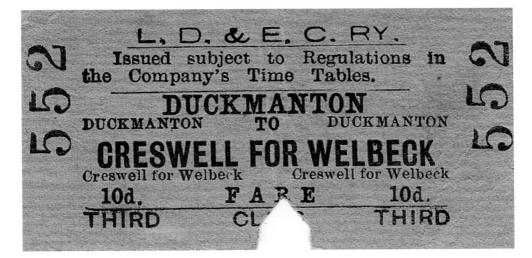

L. D. & E. C. RY.
Issued subject to Regulations in the Company's Time Tables.
DUCKMANTON
DUCKMANTON TO DUCKMANTON
CRESWELL FOR WELBECK
Creswell for Welbeck   Creswell for Welbeck
10d.   FARE   10d.
THIRD   CLASS   THIRD

552   552

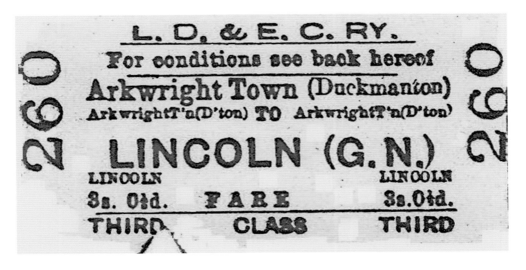

L. D. & E. C. RY.
For conditions see back hereof
Arkwright Town (Duckmanton)
ArkwrightT'n(D'ton) TO ArkwrightT'n(D'ton)
LINCOLN (G.N.)
LINCOLN   LINCOLN
3s. 0½d.   FARE   3s. 0½d.
THIRD   CLASS   THIRD

260   260

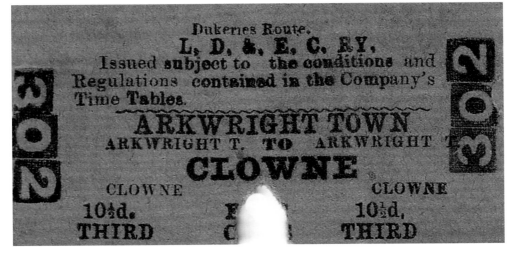

Dukeries Route.
L. D. & E. C. RY.
Issued subject to the conditions and Regulations contained in the Company's Time Tables.
ARKWRIGHT TOWN
ARKWRIGHT T. TO ARKWRIGHT T.
CLOWNE
CLOWNE   CLOWNE
10½d.   FARE   10½d.
THIRD   CLASS   THIRD

302   302

GCR Robinson A5 2-6-4T 69812 blows off excess steam as it waits to depart from Arkwright Town with the 9.35 a.m. Lincoln to Chesterfield on 14 October 1950. Introduced to service in November 1912 as GCR 452, it became LNER 5452 in 1924 and 9812 in 1946. It would end its days at Colwick Depot in July 1959. (*R. J. Buckley/Author's collection*)

Arkwright Town station slumbers in 1951 just before closure. Notice Arkwright Town Junction signal box in the right distance: the 1939 staff returns for Arkwright Town Junction showed that Arthur Stamp and John Frederick Turner were Class 5 signalmen here. (*Author's collection*)

On 17 June 1961, the RCTS ran the North Derbyshire Railtour, utilising two-car Derby Heavyweight DMU (later Class 114) 50036+56036. It is seen here in the platform at Arkwright Town, with the participants wandering around the weed-covered station. (*Alan Rowles collection*)

Arkwright Colliery

In LNER days, Arkwright Colliery was established to the east of Calow Main Colliery by the Arkwright Coal Co., a subsidiary of the Staveley Co. Another drift mine, it accessed the Waterloo seam in 1938, and connected the workings to Calow Colliery. Expanded into the Sitwell seam in 1943–1944 and later the First Waterloo, the Calow drifts were used for the ventilation and supply roadways for large machinery into Arkwright Colliery. A 20-foot diameter vertical shaft was started around 1943, but was never completed, halting at only 30 yards deep in 1950. After nationalisation in 1947, many upgrades followed, including a new stockyard, extension to the pit head baths, a new control centre and a new coal preparation plant, with the most significant new investment being a new drift in 1973. The highest output of 708,523 tons was achieved in 1972–1973. Arkwright Colliery closed on 21 January 1988 and the drifts at both Arkwright and Calow were sealed by that April.

Markham Junction

From Arkwright, the line then had a mostly downhill grade. Once the GCR had taken over the LD&ECR, they would build Arkwright Town Junction, just beyond Arkwright Station, which, via a series of other junctions, would make a connection to

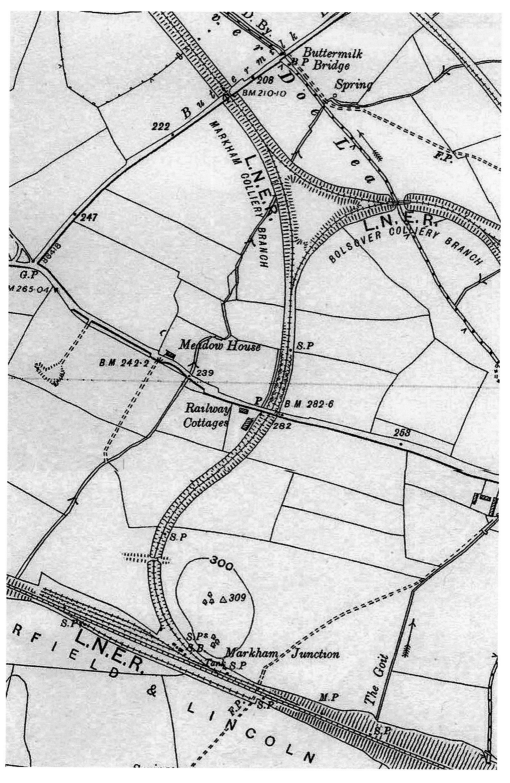

the GCR main line to London at Duckmanton Junctions. After this came another of the previously mentioned diversions of the route: the original proposed route was to the north of Bolsover, while the constructed route was to the south.

Almost 1 mile later came Markham Junction, an east-facing connection to Markham and Bolsover collieries. Sidings were laid on the Up and Down sides, and it served four collieries in its heyday: Markham Nos 1–3 and Bolsover Colliery. To control the connection and sidings, Markham Junction signal box was opened on 7 October 1897. This was as far as Great Eastern Railway coal trains worked along the line in the LD&ECR days.

Above: Markham Junction signal box opened on 7 October 1897, and contained a fifty-six-lever frame with forty-eight worked levers. Closing in 1954, its frame was not removed until 1959. These photos are dated May 1929 and show signalman Albert Robert Sarjeant wearing the flat cap on the stairs. Albert was the resident signalman there from the 1920s to the 1940s. Notice the revolving ground disc on its raised stand, adjacent to the box steps. The images are courtesy of Kevin Medford, the grandson of Albert Sarjeant, whose mother Gladys (Albert's daughter) passed them to him. (*Kevin Medford collection*)

Opposite: An extract from a map of Markham Junction and the triangular access to Bolsover Colliery, the route towards Markham Colliery heads straight on. Markham Junction signal box is at the bottom. (*Crown Copyright 1938/Author's collection*)

Above left: Signalman Albert Robert Sarjeant is now seen in the doorway, along with two of the shunting staff. Judging by the open windows and harsh shadows, it looks like a warm summer's day. The Opening of Signal Boxes Register for June 1953 showed the box was open from 5.50 a.m. to 9.30 p.m. on weekdays; it also showed that Absolute Block Regulations were worked between Arkwright Town and Markham Junction, with One Engine in Steam Regulations from there to Chesterfield Market Place. (*Kevin Medford collection*)

Above right: Markham Junction was the branch to serve the collieries at Bolsover and Markham, as well as the branch that connected with the Midland Railway line to Bolsover. To work the short section of line between the small signal box at the LD&ECR sidings at Markham Colliery and MR Signal box, there was a tablet section. In March 2013, a Tyers No. 6 single-line tablet engraved with 'MARKHAM COLLIERY MR-MARKHAM COLLIERIES LD&EC' and made of brass and steel was sold at auction. This is a remarkable survivor. (*Author's collection*)

Below: A Great Central Railway track diagram of Markham Junction signal box, dated 29 June 1922. This diagram is from the same period as the photos, which suggests that the rotating disc in the photo could be the No. 39 signal. (*Author's collection*)

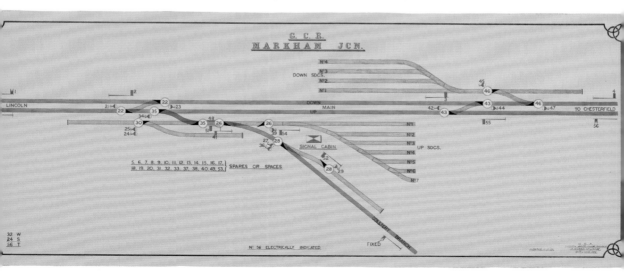

Markham Colliery Branch

As in most cases, the railways provided a workman's service to the collieries, and the MR ran trains to Markham Colliery from 1886 to 1931. The LD&ECR also introduced a workman's train service to Markham and Bolsover collieries.

A handbill in the National Archives at Kew (RAIL 931/12) dated 1910 appears to have been issued because the night-shift trains were being withdrawn to Markham Colliery; it also reveals that there were three colliery workers' halts on the former LD&ECR section of the GCR. The three halts were served by a service between Chesterfield Market Place and Markham Colliery. It is presumed that the coaching stock used on the service remained at Markham during the day, with the loco and crew being engaged in the meantime on coal workings. The 'non-public' stopping places were at Calow Junction Halt, which would have been at Cock Alley, about ¼ mile west of Duckmanton Tunnel where the colliery line diverged south of the main line.

Trains would then have had to reverse at Markham Junction to reach the next stop at Bolsover Colliery Halt. This would probably have been situated at the Railway Cottages, where the line passed under what is now the A632 Chesterfield Road, although it could possibly have been at the triangular junction between the Markham and Bolsover colliery branches, slightly further north.

Markham Colliery was the end of the LD&EC's branch, but, as stated, the MR also had a connection, as did the MS&LR (later GCR), which reached this colliery from the north. By 1885, Markham No. 1 colliery was in full production and, in 1886, Markham No. 2 was sunk into the Deep Soft seam at a depth of 504 yards from the surface—they were named after Charles Markham, a Staveley Co. director.

A ticket for a third-class workman's weekly return from Chesterfield Market Place to Markham Colliery, dated 27 March 1911. (*Glynne Waite collection*)

The 6-foot-thick Top Hard seam was the most productive in the area and the colliery expanded rapidly, with ventilation becoming a problem as faces were some considerable way out from the shafts. By 1919, the workings were out as far as Palterton, and it was decided to sink another shaft at Doe Lea Bridge; this was officially Markham No. 5 shaft, but was more generally known as the 'Palterton Air Shaft'. During the 1980s, a new shaft inset was made for the production of coal from the Second Waterloo seam, but a new drift to the surface from the number two pit bottom to free up the shaft coaling bottleneck did not get past the planning stage. The colliery finally closed in April 1993.

The Bolsover Colliery Company

The Bolsover Colliery Company was founded in 1889 by Emerson Bainbridge, who secured a lease from the Duke of Portland for land at Bolsover in Derbyshire, and began sinking shafts in 1891. Bainbridge secured the rights to mine coal at Creswell in 1894, followed by a further lease of land at Crown Farm near Mansfield in 1899. Subsequent leases were secured from Earl Manvers and Lord Savile, allowing collieries to be established at Rufford, Clipstone and Thoresby in Nottinghamshire, where coal was reached in 1913, 1922, and 1928 respectively. Coal was first produced at Bolsover in 1891, and by 1901, the colliery was winning 2,700 to 3,000 tons of coal daily. In July 1901, 3,001 tons was delivered to the surface in one day, a world record for coal production at the time. In 1947, the National Coal Board took over all the company's collieries, established an Area HQ at Bolsover and worked the colliery until its closure in 1993.

Doe Lea Viaduct

Still heading east, the line then crossed over the 70-foot-high, 370-foot-long, eight-arch Doe Lea (or Bolsover) Viaduct, which crossed the MR's Seymour Junction–Pleasley branch and the River Doe Lea. It was constructed of red bricks from the Bathurst Brickyard at Palterton (later Byron Bricks), with blue Staffordshire brick facings, although care was taken during construction to build substantial footings 25 foot below the surface. Sitting on a concrete pad, the viaduct suffered with subsidence problems in later years, and was said to be unstable and unsafe. After the line had closed, the viaduct was due to be demolished, and there were two failed attempts made to blow it up using explosives on 24 August 1952: the first at 8.15 a.m. resulted in two full piers and two halves of piers left standing. The second attempt at 9.50 a.m. fared no better; it was finally demolished by the use of bulldozers. The explosives process was filmed and the footage later used in a commercial war film, being used to represent the blowing up of a bridge in wartorn France.

Bolsover Viaduct. The MR Doe Lea Valley line from Bolsover Castle station (behind the camera) to Glapwell runs beneath the viaduct, and Bolsover Station Outer Home semaphore signal can just be discerned on this line. The LD&ECR Bolsover station would have been to the left, with Chesterfield to the right. The viaduct is long gone, having been demolished by the army on 24 August 1952. (*Author's collection*)

Bolsover Station

Shortly after the viaduct came Bolsover Station, which had the distinction of having the first level crossing along the route. Unfortunately, it was also the scene of several accidents involving child fatalities. The worst was on 24 December 1910, and an extract from the coroner's inquest report on January 1915 stated:

> From evidence given in this latter case it appears that about 5.15 p.m. on Saturday 24 December, some fifteen children were gathered at the gates on the south or Carr Vale side of the railway, waiting for a Down train, which was then approaching Bolsover station from the west, to pass. This train was travelling on the line of rails furthest from the side where the children were assembled. While this train was passing over the crossing, a goods train belonging to the Great Northern Railway Company approached the crossing from the opposite direction, this being the line of rails nearest the children. As soon as the first train had passed the crossing, the children started to run across, none of them apparently having noticed the approach of the other train, which dashed into the middle of them and scattered them in all directions, with the result that three were killed and three were seriously injured. No blame was attached to the driver of the goods train, the engine of which was running tender first, as two witnesses were able to give clear evidence that he whistled continuously as he was approaching the crossing, and was not running at any undue

speed. He was quite unaware of the disaster that had occurred, and continued on his journey without stopping.

To try and prevent further tragedy, there were suggestions that the footbridge should be moved from the centre of the platforms to the crossing end of the station, but this was discounted, as it was thought it would encourage more children to that end of the station. Instead, a subway was constructed beneath the line in late 1911 and the footbridge dispensed with. Unfortunately, even this did not stop the tragedies, as another child fatality occurred in 1923.

Bolsover had three sidings on the Up side: one of these was for the Bolsover Home Grown Fruit Preserving Company Ltd, whose premises were adjacent being served by a rail side loading dock. The factory was supplied by locally grown fruit for preserving and jams, particularly strawberries; other fruit came by rail from Wisbech and the Fens. In addition to making jam, the factory bottled fresh fruit, especially blackcurrants and bilberries, and made mincemeat in the winter. Coal for the factory came from Bolsover

Bolsover was served by another station on the MR Doe Lea Valley line, which was also just called 'Bolsover', but no distinction was made between the two until after nationalisation in 1948, with the LD&ECR 'Bolsover' becoming 'Bolsover South' from 25 September 1950. This station had the distinction of having one of the two level crossings on the entire route, and it was to be the scene of many accidents as people crossed the line there. In this shot, a view towards Chesterfield in the LD&ECR days, the level crossing can be discerned at the far end of the platform. There are seventeen members of staff, track workers and members of the public in this image, while the poster on the wall advertises Anglers Tickets for sale. In 1939, the stationmaster was Harold Hemsworth, William Edward Ball was a porter guard, and Francis Geoffrey Cutts was a lad porter. (*Nadin's Series postcard, Derek Talbot collection*)

LD&ECR class 'C' (LNER G3) 0-4-4T 1150B pauses at Bolsover in this undated shot. Six class 'C' locomotives were designed for the LD&ECR by Kitson's of Leeds, and were built in 1897 and 1898. The class 'C's were unique as the only true passenger type owned by the LD&ECR; they were used on the main line between Lincoln and Chesterfield, but also worked into Sheffield (Midland) station. During GCR ownership, many of this class carried duplicate numbers with suffixes of 'B' or 'C'. All were eventually renumbered with unique numbers during the LNER renumbering scheme of 1924. The class were withdrawn between 1931 and 1935. (*Author's collection*)

A photo taken on 26 August 1912 during the flash floods that plagued the Carr Vale area. This is the view towards Lincoln from the Dock Siding, the photographer's actions being observed by many local people and staff. Stood on the main line is a Great Eastern Railway 0-6-0 tender loco with what looks like a 'stovepipe' chimney, while in the loop is an LD&ECR tank loco. The GER had running powers to Arkwright Colliery, so maybe this train originated there. Bolsover signal box oversees the area, and the steel girder span footbridge bridge in the distance had a span of 85 feet and a height of 15 foot. (*Author's collection*)

The Lincoln-based C12 4-4-2T 7381 sets off towards Langwith, passing the signal box. To the left of the loco is a post for the collecting of single line tokens during periods when Bolsover Tunnel was undergoing maintenance and one of the tracks was out of use. At these times, the line between Bolsover and Scarcliffe would be worked as a single line and tokens would be issued to the driver of each train to ensure only one train was in the section at one time. As for the loco, this was GNR 1528, which became LNER 4528, then 7381, before its BR number of 67381 was acquired in 1948. It would be withdrawn in 1952. (*H. K. Boulter/Author's collection*)

Bolsover station on 30 March 1951 as Tuxford-allocated Class 04/7 63588 storms through with a loaded train. The station slumbers, but would be put to death later that year on 3 December after the closure of Bolsover Tunnel. (*H. B. Priestley/Author's collection*)

Colliery and glass jars from factories in Chesterfield and Worksop. The company ceased production in 1959, and the following year the factory, together with part of the old LD&ECR goods yard, was acquired by the urban district council for industrial development. The factory was later occupied by a business manufacturing lubricants.

After Bolsover, the line climbed and passed through the 1 mile and 864 yards long Bolsover tunnel, which was to cause many problems in its construction, being plagued with water and subsidence whilst it was being constructed and throughout its life. The tunnel yielded around 200,000 gallons of water each day and, although it was an undesirable by-product, this was used as the main source of water for several local villages. To cope with this water, modifications were made to the original design, including a special brick lining up to 3 feet thick and a long invert at the eastern end of the tunnel, which was built on a continuous gradient of 1-in-120 up in an easterly direction and had two ventilation shafts, the deepest being 205 feet.

A view of C12 4-4-2T 7381, which is either backing its train into the sidings or departing the siding and heading towards Bolsover Tunnel—the ground signal is in the 'off' position, suggesting the latter. Bolsover Tunnel was 2,624 yards long and suffered with subsidence and water problems for many years: indeed, a special tunnel gang was employed seven days a week to keep it maintained and under observation. In 1942, the LNER deemed the Up line unsafe due to water erosion of the north wall, so they lifted the track and slewed the Down line. Key token single line working was introduced between Bolsover Station and Scarcliffe signal boxes. A leather pouch would be handed to the driver by the signalman containing that 'key token', ensuring that his was the only train on that stretch of line. (*H. K. Boulter/Author's collection*)

As viewed from the footbridge, this is a general view of the station area looking towards Chesterfield on 25 September 1947. The Saxby-and-Farmer-built Bolsover signal box has a large consignment of drainage pipes next to it. To the right of the picture are the Bolsover Preserving Factory and its associated sidings, while Ivatt Class C12 4-4-2T No 7381 pauses in the station on a four-coach Chesterfield to Lincoln train. In October 1939, there was a class 5 signal box and the signalmen were Rupert Westbury, Ernest Oldham, and Arthur Mather. The box closed along with the line on 2 December 1951. (*H. K. Boulter/Author's collection*)

Scarcliffe

Emerging from Bolsover Tunnel next came Scarcliffe station, which was built as an island platform. This station and Dukeries Junction were the only two along the line to have island platforms and wooden buildings.

Continuing on from Scarcliffe a small level crossing was provided over a farm track that led from Rectory Road (in Upper Langwith) to Langwith Wood. Although the farm track would later be diverted over Bridge No. 30, the level crossing remained *in situ* until after 1907, as it was still shown on line diagrams that the GCR produced after takeover.

After this, the line entered a limestone cutting before passing beneath Bridge No. 31, Common Lane, after which came a short embankment beneath which was a cattle creep (No. 32) and then an occupation crossing. Then came another long limestone cutting with bridges over, and at the end of this was Recreation Road Bridge, followed by Langwith Junction Station. Here, the Beighton Branch trailed into the Up side from the north. Prior to the arrival of the LD&ECR, Langwith Junction was a greenfield site on the outskirts of the village of Shirebrook, the village of Langwith itself being a couple of miles away.

Above: George Hunt was the Scarcliffe stationmaster and here he is resplendent in frock coat, posing in his office. The family lived in the newly built four-bedroom house situated at the entrance to the station premises. The 1901 Census showed him at the age of thirty-six as a railway traffic inspector; his wife, Alice, was also thirty-six; and they had two children, four-year-old Jessie Maude and one-year-old Kathleen Mary. By 1909, he was the stationmaster; however, Alice died in February 1910 and was buried at St Leonard church on 16 February 1910. The 1911 Census showed George as a widower, but there was also a son aged seven named George Eric. Sadly, Eric and his siblings would have to grow up without their mum. (*Author's collection*)

Below: Here are George and family posing at Scarcliffe. From left to right, the children are Jessie, Kathleen, and Eric—however, according to one caption to a photo, the lady is George's second wife, the former Miss Askew. If that is true, then he did not hang about after Alice's death. The station's island platform contained gardens of roses and Mesembryanthemums and was the recipient of many 'Best Kept Station' awards, which were framed and proudly displayed in the waiting room. This was quite the achievement, considering the number of stations between there and Lincoln. The 1939 staff returns showed that Harry Field and William Ball were porter signalmen here. Notice the signal box in the background: this was a Saxby and Farmer design that opened on 7 October 1897. It had a twenty-four lever Saxby and Farmer frame, and its final signalman was Trevor Skirrey, whose story can be found on the 'Forgotten Relics' website at www.forgottenrelics.co.uk. (*Author's collection*)

A5 4-6-2T 69812 is seen as it works the 12.45 p.m. Lincoln to Chesterfield at Scarcliffe on 5 August 1950. Designed by Robinson and entering service as GCR 452 on 30 November 1912, it was withdrawn on 7 July 1959 from Colwick (40E). (*R. J. Buckley/Author's collection*)

Former MS&LR Parker N5 0-6-2T 69323 is seen at Scarcliffe on 5 August 1950, with the 1.15 p.m. Chesterfield to Lincoln train. This loco entered service in June 1899 as No. 899, becoming LNER 5899 then 9323, before gaining its BR number in 1950. Allocated to Langwith Junction at the time of the photo, it would end its days at Darnall 39B in November 1956. (*R. J. Buckley/Author's collection*)

We are now in 1951 and close to the end of operation of the line from Chesterfield. As viewed from the signal box, the driver of A5 4-6-2T 69812, working a Chesterfield to Lincoln service, prepares to drop the token pouch on to the receiving post at Scarcliffe, after working through Bolsover Tunnel during single line working on 18 May 1951. (*H. B. Priestley/Author's collection*)

A5 4-6-2T 68915 is seen *en route* from Langwith Junction to Chesterfield. The loco has just passed beneath Bridge 30, a minor road bridge that led from Upper Langwith to Langwith Wood. The photographer is stood on a small foot crossing that was originally the minor road, which was closed by the LD&ECR when the line was built, the bridge replacing it. Remarkably, most of the bridge is still *in situ* today and it is possible to see where the minor road ran down from it to the track level. The line of concrete fence posts on the right is also still *in situ*. (*Author's collection*)

Langwith Junction

Langwith Junction station consisted of four platforms: two for the Beighton Branch and two for the Chesterfield lines. Passengers had the luxury of a refreshment room in the main station building, which was built in the standard modular style, and the Langwith Junction signalmen would warn passengers of the arrival of a train by ringing a bell. This box was Class 1 rated and staffed continually until its dying years, when it closed on Sundays. There was a long lattice work public footbridge spanning the station, which also gave access to the platforms. Replaced in 1960 with a utilitarian steel design, it was removed in the spring of 1986 and transported away for use elsewhere. Although not in Shirebrook, the station was renamed Shirebrook North by the LNER in 1924.

Leen Valley Line

In 1898, the Great Northern Railway (GNR) connected to the LD&ECR at Langwith Junction with its Leen Valley extension, this joining the LD&ECR line alongside the engine shed and facing towards Chesterfield, twelve chains east of the station. The high embankment built to allow it to join the LD&ECR neatly divided Shirebrook village in half, and the GNR station later became known as Shirebrook South, where passenger services began on 1 November 1901. A connection would be established just south of the station to Shirebrook Colliery.

In 1896, the Shirebrook Colliery Company began sinking two shafts, each 18 foot in diameter, at Shirebrook, reaching coal at a depth of about 600 yards. In 1908, 1,345 men were employed underground and 282 men on the surface and, by 1909, the Shirebrook Colliery Company was exporting coal to France, Russia, Italy, Spain, Germany, Norway, and Sweden. The colliery produced its first 1 million tons of coal in 1970 and over 1.7 million tons by 1986–87, a North Derbyshire Area record. The colliery merged with Pleasley Colliery in 1983, before closing in April 1993.

This is where we leave the description of the route, which will be continued in Volume Two.

Ten Years of Independence

Chesterfield was the only town of any size that the LD&ECR served, although Sheffield was also reached via a roundabout route. Passenger services grew from 277,615 carried in 1897 to 536,491 in 1905, while freight tonnages, the main reason for its existence, grew from 477,374 in 1897 to 2,317,714 in 1905, giving gross receipts of £42,000 and £142,000 respectively. However, the hopes of the directors were never going to be fulfilled and, as a result, after much debate and disagreement, it was decided that the company should be offered for sale. Initially, it was to be offered to the GNR in November 1905, but they would not accept the LD&ECR proposals—

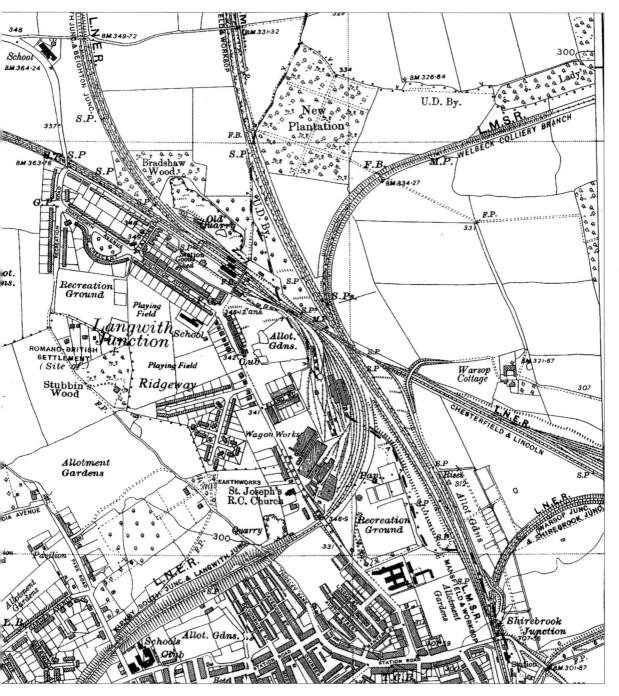

OS Map of the Langwith Junction area in 1945, quite a maze of trackwork which has mostly gone now. The route to Chesterfield heads off top left, with the Beighton Branch centre top. The Midland Railway line Nottingham to Worksop heads more or less centre top to bottom right, with the LMS Welbeck Colliery branch going off right. The GNR line to Shirebrook South and Nottingham goes off bottom centre and the Warsop curve and beginning of Warsop Yards are on the right.

What looks like a staged photo taken at Langwith Junction station around 1900. It shows an LD&ECR 'C' class loco, (Nos 15 or 16) in the Beighton line on Platform 3, with a couple of coaches. The platform has a good selection of observers, but the footbridge has even more, most of whom seem to be children. Langwith Junction station gave its name to the adjacent steam locomotive depot and the settlement that grew up around it. It was renamed Shirebrook North by the LNER on 2 June 1924, despite not being in Shirebrook; however, the signal box retained its Langwith Junction name. The 1939 staff returns for the station showed that the stationmaster was Henry William Gasson, with relief porter Harold Hassop and porters John William Howard, Arthur William Green, and Thomas Templeman. William Meredeth Gaunt was signal lampman. Langwith Junction signal box was staffed by signalman Class 1 William Franks and William Henry Kitchen, with district relief Class 1 signalmen William Stevens and Albert John Brown (*Neil Baker collection*)

The running in board states 'Langwith Junction for Shirebrook' in this image from around 1910. The station looks very quiet—in reality, it would never be really busy. (*Author's collection*)

The photographer is observed as he takes this image of Langwith Junction around 1910. On the left, two staff members loiter in the doorway of the small building, while at least two passengers look on from the platform. What looks like possibly a GNR locomotive is in the platform on a short goods train, while on the right a gang of plate layers, complete with their trolley, stop to watch proceedings. The trolley has a load of barrels on board. Langwith Junction signal box is in the centre of the image: notice the bar style point rodding in the foreground, along with No. 42 Ground Disc. (*Author's collection*)

After arrival at Shirebrook North from Lincoln, C13 4-4-2T 67437 shunts its train of Thompson non-gangway coaches, a Brake Composite, Third and Brake Third, ready to form its return working to Lincoln. Introduced to service as GCR 114 in May 1905, and becoming LNER 7437 in 1946, it would be withdrawn in August 1957. (*T. G. Hepburn/Author's collection*)

Above: C13 4-4-2T 67437 is seen again, this time on the 10.52 a.m. Shirebrook North to Lincoln at a cold Shirebrook North on 19 February 1955. Although it looks like the line towards Chesterfield is still open, in reality it stops at some buffer stops just out of view, as the line onwards had closed four years previous. (*R. J. Buckley/Author's collection*)

Below: Class 04/2 63847 on the 3.25 p.m. freight from Staveley to Langwith Junction arrives at Shirebrook North on 22 August 1951. The short train consists of a motley collection of twelve wagons of coal, ranging from five and seven-plank wooden ones to a steel-bodied variant at the rear of the train. Notice the large 'Shirebrook North for Langwith' running-in board and the three-plank wagon with flapping sheets behind the tender. This loco was built by the North British Locomotive Company, Glasgow, Works No. 22139, and introduced to service as ROD No. 2046 in May 1919. Taken on by the LNWR and renumbered to 2837 in September 1919, it went back to the ROD in August 1921. Stored until 1924, it was then taken into care of the LNER and became LNER 6290 in August 1924, allocated to Thornton Junction. It became a Langwith Junction engine on 28 July 1943 and was transferred to Doncaster in October 1946. Renumbered 3847 in December 1946, it moved to Frodingham in 1948, before becoming BR 63847 in September 1949. Moved again to Staveley on 18 March 1951, where it was based at the time of this photo, it would end its days in May 1959, being cut up at Gorton Works. (*R. J. Buckley/Author's collection*)

Above: The recently overhauled Class 04/2 2-8-0 63842 works a Class 'J' freight consisting of coal empties off the Beighton Branch at Shirebrook North on 10 March 1961. Another ROD loco, this one was built by NBL in February 1919, too late for War Service. It became ROD 1998, but was purchased by the LNER, becoming 6257 in February 1924. Renumbered 3842 in 1946, on nationalisation it was given an 'E' prefix as E3842, before gaining its final BR number of 63842 on 31 March 1951. Based at Langwith Junction in October 1926, it would move to Colwich, followed by spells at Doncaster and Mexborough, before returning to Langwith Junction from 2 July 1950. It went into Gorton Works for a general overhaul in 1961, where it was fitted with boiler No. 22115, returning to Langwith on 10 February 1961, just a month before this image was taken. It was condemned on 4 April 1965 and dispatched to Cashmore's at Great Bridge for disposal. (*Lawson Little/Author's collection*)

Below: As another load of coal comes off the Beighton line behind a tender first Class 04, so J11 0-6-0 64379 pilots 04 2-8-0 63715 on Down goods off the main line towards the Beighton line on 10 April 1954. The train consist includes a brand new white painted tank wagon, maybe a product of W. H. Davies of Langwith Junction. (*R. J. Buckley/Author's collection*)

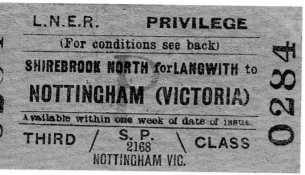
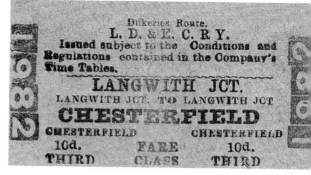

Langwith Junction was renamed Shirebrook North by the LNER in 1924, and these tickets reflect that change. The LD&ECR one is Langwith Jct., while the LNER one is Shirebrook North for Langwith. (*Glynne Waite collection*)

A special visitor in the shape of A3 4-6-2 4472 *Flying Scotsman* on 18 April 1964. It was working the Great Central Railway Rail Tour, this section of the tour being from Sheffield Victoria–Woodhouse East Junction–Killamarsh Junction–Clowne South–Shirebrook North, where it is seen taking water from 10.44 a.m. to 10.50 a.m., before heading off via the Leen Valley Line to Kirkby South Junction–Annesley and Nottingham Victoria to London Marylebone. (*Derek Talbot*)

Above: Having passed Shirebrook North, B1 4-6-0 61377 is now making a lot of smoke as it storms onto the former GNR Leen Valley Line. The train is about to pass beneath Langwith Road Bridge, and the wagons on the left are in the sidings of W. H. Davis Wagon Works. (*Author's collection*)

Below: English Electric Type 1 D8198 is seen passing the site of Langwith Sidings signal box on Saturday 4 May 1968 with 5M29, the 11.20 a.m. Saturdays only working from Wadsley Bridge Batchelor's canning factory to the Oddicroft Metal Box factory at Sutton-in-Ashfield. Langwith Sidings signal box was roughly on the right of the image. This box opened on 24 April 1901 and closed *c*. 1912. It was used to gain access to the exchange sidings that had been laid here. A line was proposed to be built from Langwith Sidings to Warsop Junction, this giving the GCR/GNR a direct route towards Nottingham from the Lincoln direction without the need to use the Midland Railway via Mansfield. The opening of the Mansfield Railway from Clipstone to Kirkby South Junction in 1913 made the need for this short curve redundant, and it seems as though this is why the box closed shortly afterwards. (*Syd Hancock*)

With the destination board reading Shirebrook, Great Northern Railway Sturrock 0-4-2T No. 242 has arrived at Shirebrook Station in this undated photo. The first series (Nos 241–50) of these locomotives were built between 1865 and 1867 for working the Great Northern trains over the Metropolitan Railway. They had 16 × 22 inch cylinders and coupled wheels that were 5 foot 6 inches and reported as being 'none too steady at the rear end'. (*Author's collection*)

A second view of Great Northern Railway Sturrock 0-4-2T No. 242 at Shirebrook, Judging by the condition of the station, which opened to goods traffic on 3 August 1901 and passengers on 1 November 1901, this could be a very early photo of it. There were ten passenger trains from Nottingham London Road station every day Monday to Friday, with extras on a Saturday, all initially terminating at Shirebrook South. From 1 February 1903, the service was extended to Chesterfield Market Place, however, this was short lived and, when the GCR took over the LD&ECR, they were terminated at Langwith Junction. Passenger services ceased on 14 September 1931, but summer excursions continued until 5 September 1964. Total closure of the line came on 6 May 1968. (*Author's collection*)

Shirebrook South signal box with a collection of staff having their photo taken on the steps. This box opened to control access to Shirebrook Colliery on 26 November 1900 and had a forty-lever frame. The colliery branch was single line, although there was an Up shunt siding adjacent that gave the appearance of double track from the junction; a wagon can be seen on the Up shunt siding to the right of the box. The colliery branch closed in 1952, all traffic then being worked via the former Midland Railway connection. The box itself closed on 24 May 1959. (*Author's collection*)

Above left: In the transition from steam period, diesel locomotives began to make themselves felt along the lines in the area: here, Brush Type 2 D5817 passes the closed Shirebrook South station with 1E98 10.31 a.m. from Skegness on 11 August 1962. This loco became 31285 and is still around today, formerly employed by Network Rail on test trains painted in all-over yellow; it was later sold on to Harry Needle. (*John S. Gilks*)

Above right: After crossing the large embankment that split Shirebrook village, K3 2-6-0 61975 arrives at Shirebrook North off the Leen Valley line with the 9.48 a.m. Nottingham to Cleethorpes special on 21 April 1957. (*Author's collection*)

as a result, the GCR, who had been one of the line's fiercest opponents, came into the equation and snatched the line from beneath the GNR's noses, announcing at the end of 1905 that they would take over the company from 1 January 1907. The LD&ECR enjoyed just ten years of independent life before being taken over by the GCR, who then set about the construction of connections between the GCR Main line at Duckmanton and the LD&ECR line at Arkwright Town; this was later followed by a connection between the GCR main line and the LD&ECR at Killamarsh.

Duckmanton Junctions

The Duckmanton connections consisted of a double-line connection that commenced at a point on the LD&ECR twenty-eight chains east of Arkwright Town Station, and had junctions with the GCR Main Line both to the north and south. The GCR's hope in connecting the lines was to enable them to carry coal from the LD&ECR's catchment area to markets further south, notably London. They also foresaw the possibility of traffic from their intended Immingham Dock (which would open in 1912) having an alternative route for coal from the GCR's Derbyshire catchment area.

Duckmanton North Junction was an ordinary double junction at a point on the GCR Main Line 2 miles and 23 chains south of Staveley Town station. Duckmanton South Junction, which left the northern connection at a point 44 chains away from the connection with the LD&ECR line, was also a double junction, but it differed from the north junction in that the double line connection was effected by means of a 'flying' junction. Commencing from the LD&ECR, the line at Arkwright Town Junction was first on a bank nine chains in length; it then ran into a cutting for 20 chains before crossing under the Chesterfield–Bolsover road (now the A632). From this point, the line was on a bank thirty-six chains in length, the maximum height of which was 60 foot.

The line then crossed over Works Lane and effected a junction with the GCR main line in a shallow cutting at Duckmanton East Junction. The southern junction at Duckmanton commenced on the 60-foot bank and a connection with the GCR main line was effected by means of a line that ran parallel alongside the main line for a distance of 15 chains, the cutting being widened to allow this. The 'flying' junction crossed the GCR main line by means of a steel girder bridge with a skew span of 84 foot, allowing for four tracks beneath, and a small skew span of 21 foot and 9 inches, the latter crossing over an accommodation road. The line then ran in a cutting on the west side of the main line, forming a connection with the Down main line alongside the connection with the Up main line at Duckmanton South Junction.

The work was begun in June 1906 by Messrs Hutchinson and Co. of Leeds, with the southern junction at Duckmanton being opened for goods and coal traffic on 22 September 1907 and for passengers on 1 October 1907.

The junction provision far exceeded the traffic it ever carried, being laid out and signaled to passenger standards. A 'fast' passenger service was tried from Lincoln to Nottingham, connecting with expresses to Marylebone but this took two hours to Nottingham compared with the MR's time of under an hour, and five hours to

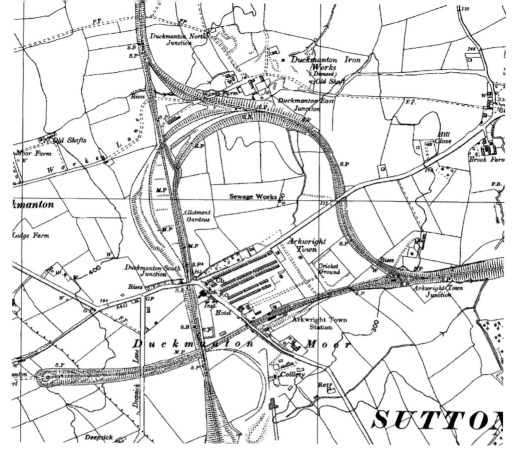

Above: This map shows the Duckmanton connections. The GCR Main line runs top to bottom, and the Duckmanton North and South Junctions can be seen. The LD&ECR runs left to right, with Arkwright Town station being bottom centre. The junction with the LD&ECR was controlled from Arkwright Town Junction box. Also on the map is Arkwright Colliery, which opened in 1938. (*Crown Copyright 1953 Author's collection*)

Below: 04/8 2-8-0 No. 63612 on the connecting spur between the LD&EC main line at Arkwright Town and the GC main line at Duckmanton North Junction, with coal from Arkwright Colliery to Staveley on 31 March 1964. In the background is Arkwright Town Junction box. This loco was GCR 8K Class No. 387, built at Gorton in 1914 and rebuilt as an 04/8 in July 1955. She would last until November 1965. (*Syd Hancock*)

In this view, Staveley Shed's 01 2-8-0 63863 slogs up the bank at the approaches to Duckmanton South Junction with up GCR main line goods for the yards at Annesley in the autumn of 1963; it will soon cross over the LD&ECR line, which runs at right angles. In the background, the line off to the left heads in a curve to cross the GCR line on the bridge; the train is hiding most of the corresponding connection from the curves to the GCR. Built for the War Department (WD) as part of the Railway Operating Division (ROD) in August 1919, this loco was numbered 2074 and originally loaned to the NER until 1921. Purchased by the LNER in 1925, it became Class 01 in September 1945 and was withdrawn in 1965. (*Syd Hancock*)

London, compared with the GNR time of three hours and thirty minutes. By 1910, this service consisted of a single carriage slipped at Leicester northbound off the 3.15 p.m. from Marylebone. It was then worked forward via Nottingham Victoria and Heath, turning east at Duckmanton Junction to Langwith Junction, where it was attached to the 6.53 p.m. all stations to Lincoln, arriving at 7.58 p.m. However, by 1922, there was no advertised passenger service using the junctions.

Unfortunately, due to the nature of the junctions, traffic from Chesterfield Market Place and Calow and Bonds Main collieries would have to reverse at Arkwright Town Junction. This was one of the reasons that led to the demise of the Calow and Bonds Main Branch, as mentioned earlier.

The simplest way of understanding the layout of the junctions was that a train travelling from the East to North would diverge at Arkwright Town Junction, pass under the A632, bear north at Duckmanton East Junction and then join the GCR main line at Duckmanton North Junction—all of this on double track. North to East traffic would reverse the process.

A train travelling from East to South would again diverge at Arkwright Town Junction, pass under the A632, bear south at Duckmanton East Junction then join the GCR main line at Duckmanton South Junction. The section from Duckmanton East Junction to Duckmanton South Junction was single track.

A train travelling from South to East would diverge off the GCR main line at Duckmanton South Junction, and then climb on a single-track arc and cross the GCR Main Line on a lattice girder bridge. It would then join the North–East line at Duckmanton East Junction, pass under the A632, and join the LD&ECR at Arkwright Town Junction.

Passenger Services

Reference to three specimen timetables (LD&ECR 1906, GCR 1910, and LNER 1938) reveals a number of interesting workings. The service to Chesterfield was quite intensive, with five services on weekdays and no less than twelve on Saturdays; several of the latter started at Clowne and reversed at Langwith Junction before continuing to Chesterfield. Incidentally, at this date the LD&ECR 'main line' was regarded as Lincoln–Langwith Junction–Sheffield, with the Chesterfield connection as a branch.

Chesterfield Market Place Platform Accommodation:

Platform 1: six coaching vehicles
Platform 2: seven coaching vehicles
There was no Platform 3, this being the release road
Platform 4: seven coaching vehicles
Platform 5: six coaching vehicles

In early British Railways livery, A5 4-6-2T 69815 brings the usual three-coach 6.25 p.m. Lincoln to Chesterfield into Shirebrook North on 7 May 1949. The coaches are an ex-GCR clerestory-style third brake, a composite, and a non-clerestory third brake. (*R. J. Buckley/ Author's collection*)

A 'four trains together' arrangement lasted for more than thirty years from Langwith Junction. Each weekday (there were never any scheduled Sunday trains on the LD&ECR), at 10.40 a.m., 2.17 p.m., 4.30 p.m., and 7.20p.m., trains would depart more or less simultaneously for Sheffield, Mansfield, Lincoln and Chesterfield. These times appeared unchanged in 1910, but by 1938 the 2.17 p.m. had disappeared, and the 7.20 p.m. to Lincoln only ran on Saturdays. By the latter date though, there were additional services to Mansfield Central via Warsop, despite the trains via the LMS still being maintained, giving a choice of five trains to Mansfield and eight on Saturdays, the last not leaving the Junction until 12.02 a.m. One working in the 1910 timetable was a through service from Langwith Junction to London Marylebone. A carriage left Lincoln at 8.10 a.m. attached to an all-stations working, arriving at Langwith Junction at 9.15 a.m. From here, it was detached and worked forward via Bolsover, then over the connection at Duckmanton onto the GCR main line to Heath, where it could make a connection there to Sheffield. Taken forward to Nottingham, it was attached to the 'Breakfast and Luncheon Corridor Express,' which arrived at Marylebone at 1.30 p.m. The return journey comprised a slip coach attached to the 3.15 p.m. ex-Marylebone and detached at Leicester, working forward by the same route as the morning service and arriving at Langwith Junction at 6.55 p.m., where it was attached to a local service which reached Lincoln at 7.58 p.m.

For a few years in the late 1920s, there was also a direct service to Nottingham via the GNR Leen Valley line, but this was withdrawn in 1931. Right up to the outbreak of the Second World War, however, Shirebrook North remained busy, with a total of nineteen daily departures (and no less than thirty-one on Saturdays), including a particularly intensive service to Chesterfield (eight trains each way, with four extra on Saturdays).

Passenger Services Cease

The Sheffield District Railway (SDR), which had been conceived as an independent route by which the LD&ECR could reach Sheffield (see Chapter Three), closed to passengers from 11 September 1939 for the duration of the Second World War, reopening briefly afterwards between 6 October 1946 and 17 March 1947. Excursions and specials trains for Mount St Mary College at Spink Hill continued along the Beighton Branch until the early 1960s, and summer Saturday specials to East Coast resorts continued to use the line until 1964.

By the end of the war, almost all the Saturday extras along the LD&ECR had also been withdrawn, leaving only seven trains to Chesterfield (plus a late evening Saturday working), three to Lincoln and just one to Mansfield, the latter running via Clipstone Junction. By 1946, with a much-improved network of local bus routes, departures from Shirebrook North (as it was then) had been reduced to six trains to Chesterfield, two of which had originated at Lincoln and one at Mansfield Central (via Warsop). There were just two trains to Lincoln and one return working to Mansfield.

Passenger services between Chesterfield Market Place and Shirebrook North ceased on 3 December 1951 due to the condition of Bolsover Tunnel. However, goods traffic

Robinson A5 4-6-2T 69804, seen at Shirebrook North working the 'School Train' on 2 September 1955; this train ran daily for local pupils attending Chesterfield Grammar School. A 'Blood and Custard' livery Gresley coach is in the adjacent platform. Built at Gorton Works and introduced to service on 31 May 1911 as GCR 169, at Grouping the loco became LNER 5169 followed by 9804, before gaining its BR number 69804. Its last shed was 38A Colwick, and it was withdrawn on 30 May 1958 and sent for disposal at Darlington Works where it was cut up in June 1958. (*Author's collection*)

N5 0-6-2T 69323 working the 4.20 p.m. from Edwinstowe passes Langwith Junction signal box as it arrives at Shirebrook North on 4 July 1953. Built as GCR 899 and introduced to service in June 1899, it became LNER 9323 in August 1946 and BR 69323 in January 1950, before being withdrawn in November 1956. (*R. J. Buckley/Author's collection*)

to Chesterfield Market Place would continue until May 1957, with access to the LD&ECR line being obtained via the curves and junctions at Duckmanton.

The last timetabled passenger train left Shirebrook North for Lincoln at 4.17 p.m. on 17 September 1955, hauled by A5 4-6-2T No. 69828; the train consisted of a Thompson three-coach set plus a couple of extra coaches for the non-existent last-day crowds. However, Edwinstowe station would remain open until 2 January 1956, when the services to Nottingham Victoria via Mansfield Central ceased, leading to the closure of Mansfield Central, Sutton-in-Ashfield Central, and Kirkby-in-Ashfield Central stations. The passenger services over the GNR Leen Valley line had ceased from 14 September 1931, but were reinstated from 20 February to 17 September 1956 to serve Sutton-in-Ashfield, as a compensation for the loss of other trains via the closed Mansfield Railway (see Volume Two for more on this railway).

The summer 1964 timetable showed a Saturdays-only service and, by the winter 1964–65 timetable, was shown merely as 'service suspended'. Summer Saturday excursion trains would continue to use the stations at Shirebrook North, Edwinstowe and Ollerton until 4 January 1965. The 1965–66 timetable dropped the route completely, although no statutory notices to withdraw the service were posted at any of the stations affected. Although the service had been on one day a week for the summer only, for several years, Shirebrook North, Warsop, Edwinstowe, and Ollerton had always been shown as

After the closure of the line between Chesterfield and Langwith in 1951, the goods yard at Chesterfield was still served by trains. To access the station, the only route was via the Duckmanton Curves off the GCR main line, then via Arkwright Town Junction to Chesterfield. Naturally, with the closure of the signal boxes along the route, a method of working had to be implemented between Arkwright Town Junction and Market Place station. This was done by the use of a staff: here we see that staff, which survives today in the Joe Clark collection. It is made of square section brass and is around 1 foot long, engraved with Arkwright Town on one face and Chesterfield M. P. on another. (*Courtesy of Joe Clark via Les Elson*)

J11 0-6-0 64389 crosses towards the Beighton Branch at Shirebrook North with a 12:38 football special from Ollerton to Wadsley Bridge on 28 April 1956, while over to the right an unidentified 04 undertakes shunting duties. The football match that day was between the home team at Hillsborough (Sheffield Wednesday), and Lincoln City, whose supporters were no doubt on this train. The score was to be a win of 5-3 for the home team—as for the loco, it would be withdrawn on 23 January 1960. (*R. J. Buckley/Author's collection*)

The last timetabled passenger train left Shirebrook North for Lincoln without ceremony at 4.17 p.m. on 17 September 1955, hauled by A5 4-6-2T 69828. The train consisted of a Thompson three-coach set plus a couple of extra coaches for the non-existent last-day crowds. Here it is waiting to depart with just a few observers. (*R. J. Buckley/Author's collection*)

Dad examines the closure notice at Shirebrook North on 10 December 1955, as his son looks on, perhaps wondering how they will get to the football matches advertised in November and December 1955, seeing as the passenger service had been withdrawn. There were, of course, special trains laid on for these matches. (*Author's collection*)

passenger stations on Eastern Region maps, and the line continued to generate excursion traffic, primarily from the Miners' Welfare coastal outings that were a feature of the time. For instance, on 9 June 1965, a twelve-coach train left Ollerton for Cleethorpes, carrying 650 members, wives and children on the annual outing of the Bilsthorpe Colliery Welfare. On the following day, four trains left Edwinstowe and Ollerton for Skegness on the Thoresby Colliery Welfare outing. On Sunday 27 June, four trains left Ollerton for Skegness on the Ollerton-Bevercotes Miners' Welfare outing. These trains were originally booked to carry 1,400 children and 1,100 adults, but later each train was extended to eleven, thirteen, thirteen, and thirteen coaches respectively so that 2,800 passengers could be carried. Even this failed to meet the demand, and buses had to be hired to carry the remainder. Most of the stock required was brought from Sheffield before the journey and returned there afterwards, but some were stabled before or after at Shirebrook North.

Line Closures

Due to the railway not purchasing the coal measures beneath its lines, there was the ever-imminent threat of the tracks subsiding owing to underground colliery workings. There were many undulations between Arkwright Town and Bolsover in particular, and increased colliery subsidence between Scarcliffe and Bolsover began to affect the safety of Bolsover Tunnel. Upon inspection about September 1948, it was found that the roof of the tunnel had sunk several inches to a dangerous position. A 10-mph speed restriction was immediately imposed, and repair work to the side walls and roof begun, as it was feared that coaches might foul the side clearance of the tunnel. Simultaneously, the Down line was centred some eighteen inches and the Up line taken out of use. Single line working was introduced through the tunnel and work began to reline the tunnel from the Bolsover end, with trains travelling on the Down line. The Up line was used for inspection trolleys which worked from the Scarcliffe side only, the other end being blocked near the tunnel entrance by a sleeper laid across the rails. As the work progressed, tentative proposals were put forward that the 9-mile stretch of line between Chesterfield and Shirebrook North should be closed to passenger traffic and buses substituted. Suggestions were also made that the Beighton Branch, which had closed to passenger traffic in 1939, should be re-opened to passenger traffic, as well as the GNR Leen Valley line. It was said that this would introduce a through route between Sheffield Victoria and Mansfield Central and a much shorter route to Nottingham from Shirebrook than that in use.

Due to the main development of the coal industry after 1907 occurring in the Mansfield area, Immingham Dock traffic would head there directly, rather than heading through the Duckmanton Junctions onto the GCR main line, and really Duckmanton Junction became a white elephant, being used on occasions for diversions, but otherwise just for local goods traffic. Arkwright Colliery opened close to the junctions in 1938 and was connected to the LD&ECR line by a sharply curving branch.

By the late 1940s it was being reported that the Chesterfield Market Place to Shirebrook section did not pay its way with regard to ordinary passenger traffic, and that the three coach trains could easily be reduced to a single carriage and there would still be no crowding. However, in August 1948, day excursions to Skegness from all stations between Bolsover and Clifton-on-Trent (except Tuxford and Dukeries Junction) were said to be extremely well-loaded with nine to ten coach loads.

All the work in Bolsover Tunnel came to nothing and the subsidence continued so much so that, as previously mentioned, passenger services ceased and the section from Chesterfield to Shirebrook North closed on 3 December 1951. The final portion of the LD&ECR main line between Chesterfield Market Place and Langwith Junction to remain in use was between Market Place and Markham Junction.

In Chesterfield, the final vestiges of track were removed from the station area in 1957–1958 and Park Road Bridge was demolished with the aid of explosives. Although the tracks were lifted, the embankment and viaduct at Horns Bridge remained intact until 1960, when the metal girder spans were removed. However, the brick uprights and arches remained in place for a time; the last arches remained until 1985, when they and the embankment to the west were swept away for road alterations.

With the closure of the LD&ECR from Markham Junction to Langwith Junction, Duckmanton Junctions had no role for any through traffic, as only local traffic was utilising them. This consisted of a daily goods service to and from Chesterfield Market Place that also served Arkwright Town, and coal from Markham No. 1, Bolsover, and Arkwright Collieries.

From March 1957, traffic ceased servicing Chesterfield Market Place with traffic working as far as Arkwright Town Station, but even this ceased on 2 February 1963. Due to the partial closure of the route, traffic from Markham Colliery to Langwith

View from the footbridge towards Bolsover Tunnel on 21 August 1952. Passenger services between Chesterfield and Langwith Junction had been discontinued early in December 1951 and, by the date of this photo, the tunnel entrance is partially bricked up and the trackwork is in the process of removal. (*H. K. Boulter/Author's collection*)

Taken around 1980, this image shows the embankment to the west of the Midland Line and the final arches of Horns Bridge over Derby Road. A Class 45 hauled express heads along the Midland line towards Chesterfield and Sheffield, while a red Morris Marina registration ORA 117P makes its way towards the camera. Road changes here in 1984–5 would see the end of the arches. (*Author's collection*)

Junction now had to be routed via Markham Junction (reverse) then Arkwright Town Junction, Duckmanton East Junction, Duckmanton North Junction, then Killamarsh South Junction (reverse) and along the LD&ECR's Beighton Branch.

As both Bolsover and Markham collieries were connected to the ex-MR Doe Lea Branch, eventually traffic ceased being sent via the LD&ECR route. Markham Junction signal box closed in 1954, and before long bufferstops were erected between Arkwright Town Junction and Markham Junction, with the branches to Bolsover and Markham Collieries lifted. As such, Arkwright Colliery was now the only source of traffic on the LD&ECR west of Langwith Junction

The closure of routes would lead to a vast simplification of the track and signalling. The two single tracks from Duckmanton South Junction to Duckmanton East Junction were lifted between autumn 1963 and February 1965 and the lattice girder flyover removed. Duckmanton North Junction to Arkwright Junction was singled, the Duckmanton East and Arkwright Town signal boxes were abolished, and all signalling was removed.

September 1966 saw the GCR main line north of Nottingham closed and the tracks south of Duckmanton North Junction lifted and track singled to the north. Traffic to serve Arkwright was now the sole user of the much-depleted route from Beighton Junction to Arkwright Colliery, with reversals at Arkwright Town Junction and again into the colliery siding.

Arkwright Town Junction box opened on 12 March 1907 with a thirty-two-lever McKenzie and Holland frame, it is seen here on 12 July 1964 after the box had closed. This is the view towards Bolsover, with the connection to the GCR on the left. By this time, the junction itself had been singled and trains for Arkwright Colliery would be using only the former LD&ECR Up main line as a head shunt, with the Down main (on the left) relegated to a siding. The connection to the GCR main line was controlled by a ground frame beyond the box. The mining subsidence which caused many problems to the rail lines in the area is evident just beyond the box and the beginnings of opencast mining operations, which finally removed all trace of the railway here, are seen behind the box. (*Syd Hancock*)

To dispense with this slow method of working, in 1973 BR built a new connection between the ex-MR Foxlow Junction to Seymour Junction line and the ex-GCR main line, through the site of Staveley Central station, and relayed the GCR Main Line from Duckmanton North Junction southwards to the bridge over the former LD&ECR line. They removed the overbridge and constructed a north to east curve where the lines had previously crossed, thereby giving direct access into Arkwright Colliery Yard without any reversals. This opened on 2 April 1973.

The section from Duckmanton North Junction southwards as far as the western A632 bridge consisted of a single track with a passing loop, this ending exactly where Duckmanton South Junction had been. With the closure of Arkwright Colliery in 1988, all the previously relaid tracks were lifted.

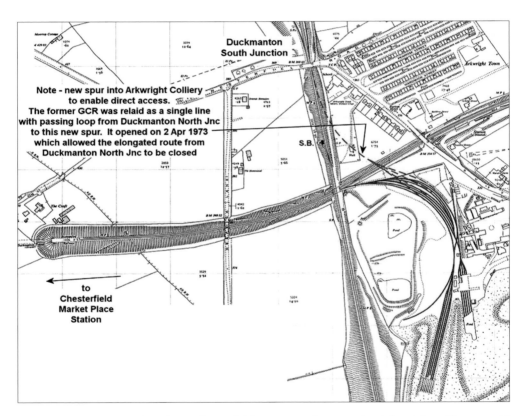

After the closure of the line from Chesterfield to Langwith, trains for Arkwright colliery would have to take the former GCR main line from Staveley as far as Duckmanton North Junction, then utilise the Duckmanton curves to Arkwright Junction. There they would have to run round, before taking the former LD&ECR line to Arkwright Town; they would take the line towards Duckmanton Tunnel and then set back into the colliery yard. Obviously, the return workings would have to be the same way, with all the attendant run rounds. To simplify matters and allow a considerable amount of track to be removed, a short link was built between the GCR main line at Duckmanton South Junction and the colliery yard, as highlighted in red on this map. This opened in 1973. (*Courtesy of Zoe Elizabeth Hunter*)

2

The Beighton Branch

Construction of the 12 miles between Langwith Junction and Beighton Junction began in 1892, with the line opening in sections. As previously mentioned, the contractors for the first section from Langwith Junction to Barlborough No. 1 Colliery Junction were Messrs S. Pearson and Son, and the first part of the branch was opened for goods on 16 November 1896, with passenger traffic to Clowne beginning on 8 March 1897.

Pearson and Son employed a large number of men for building the line between Bolsover and Chesterfield and towards Beighton and, as such, during 1893 a contractors' village was built between the MR and LD&ECR lines in the vicinity of Norwood Crossings. Extensive fitting shops were erected, along with huts for the workmen and their families, many of whom had come from as far away as Liverpool to work on the line. The children attended Whaley Thorns School. However, by 15 May 1896, the contractor's village was cleared away. In September 1897, Messrs Price and Wills were awarded the contract to extend the branch 4.5 miles from Barlborough No. 1 Colliery Junction to a new station at Killamarsh at a cost of £15,841; this opened to goods traffic on 21 September 1898 and to all traffic on 1 October 1898, while Killamarsh–Beighton Junction did not formally open for invited guests until 21 May 1900, and for goods traffic on 29 May 1900.

The MR provided platforms close to Langwith Colliery for the use of miners on their Mansfield to Worksop line, and in 1894 a petition was put forward for a station to be sited near the Whaley Road overbridge, on the Beighton Branch. On 29 June 1897, a public meeting was held, with the colliery manager Mr Bennett in the chair, to petition again for a station, particularly for the eighty miners there were said to come to the pit from Warsop. The nearest stations for the village were either at Langwith Junction or Creswell, and one of the original ideas was for a station near the Devonshire Arms public house at Upper Langwith on the main line. As it happened, none of these were ever built.

Route Details

From Langwith Junction, the line headed north, paralleling the MR Mansfield to Worksop line; the two lines were no more than a quarter of a mile apart for the first 3 miles. The line passed through a deep limestone cutting for several hundred yards after departing Langwith Junction, before reaching the location of the first colliery.

BEIGHTON, CLOWN, LANGWITH, SHIREBROOK.

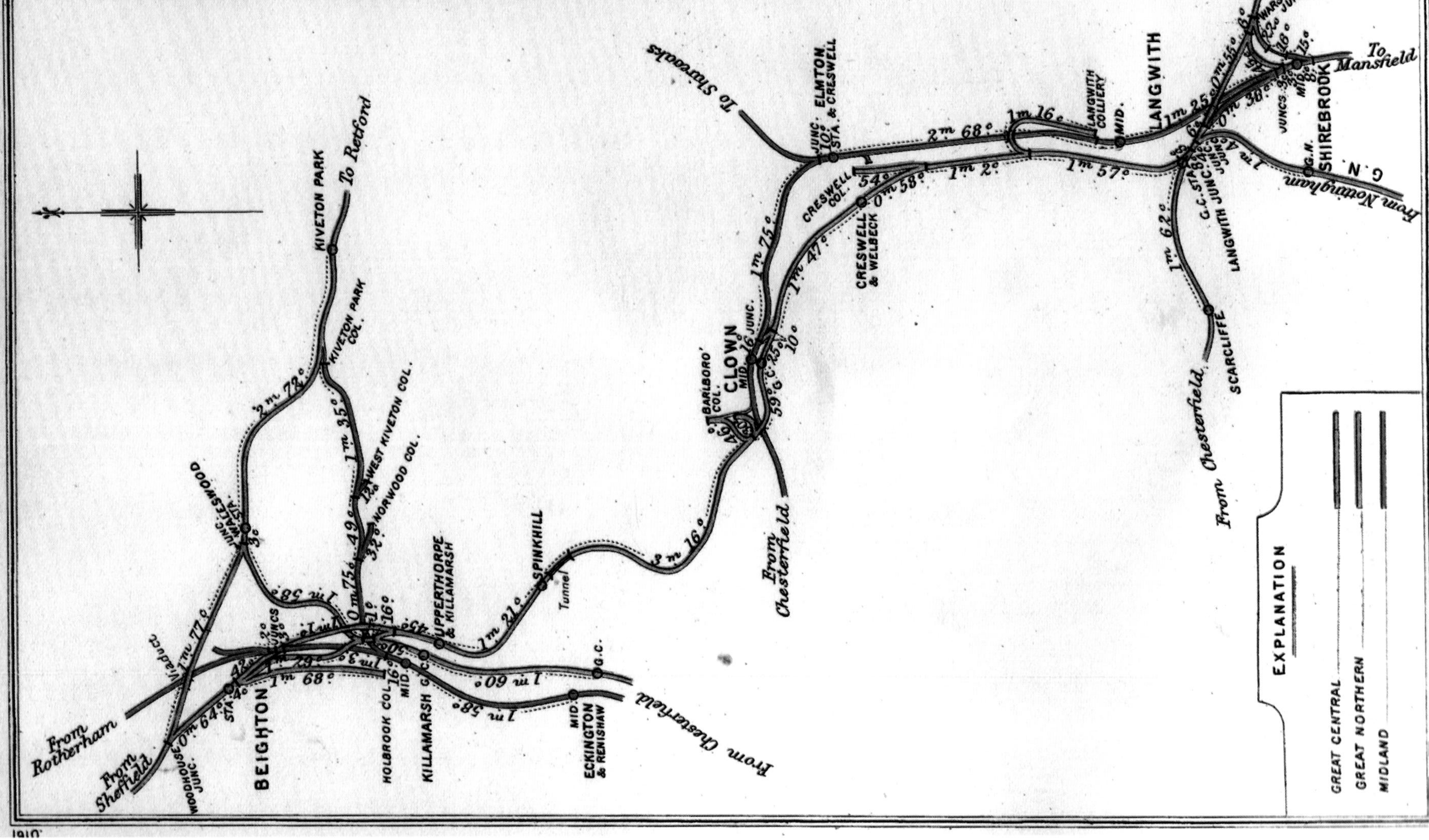

From Rotherham
From Sheffield

Viaduct
1 m 77 c
WOODHOUSE JUNC.
0 m 64 c
BEIGHTON
JUNC. WALESWOOD STA.
3 c
1 m 58 c
2 c
JUNCS
2 m 72 c
KIVETON PARK
KIVETON PARK COL.
To Retford
0 m 75 c
49 c
1 m 35 c
WEST KIVETON COL.
HOLBROOK COL.
16 c
16 c
32 c
NORWOOD COL.
MID.
KILLAMARSH G.C.
UPPERTHORPE & KILLAMARSH
1 m 58 c
1 m 60 c
1 m 21 c
SPINKHILL
Tunnel
MID.
ECKINGTON & RENISHAW
G.C.
From Chesterfield

8 m 16 c
BARLBORO' COL.
46 c
48 c
CLOWN
MID.
16 c JUNC.
1 m 75 c
To Shireoaks
From Chesterfield
59 c
25 c
10 c
1 m 47 c
CRESWELL COL.
JUNC. ELMTON STA. & CRESWELL
10 c
CRESWELL & WELBECK
0 m 58 c
34 c
2 m 68 c
1 m 2 c
1 m 16 c
1 m 57 c
LANGWITH COLLIERY
MID.
LANGWITH
From Chesterfield
1 m 62 c
SCARCLIFFE
G.C. STA.
LANGWITH JUNC.
JUNC
JUNC
1 m 25 c
0 m 55 c
To Lincoln
WARSOP MAIN JUNC.
JUNCS.
MID.
15 c
From Nottingham
G.N.
G.N.
SHIREBROOK
To Mansfield

EXPLANATION

GREAT CENTRAL
GREAT NORTHERN
MIDLAND

Above: B1 4-6-0 61405 is seen in the deep limestone cutting between Langwith Colliery Junction and Shirebrook North with a Belper to Cleethorpes special on 21 April 1957. This loco was introduced to service on 10 May 1950 to 40A Lincoln, it would last a mere 12 years before being condemned off Lincoln on 16 September 1962. Scrapping came during January 1963 at Cox and Danks of Wadsley Bridge. (*R. J. Buckley/Author's collection*)

Opposite: Railway Clearing House map dated 1910, showing the Beighton Branch and connections at Langwith Junction and Beighton Junction. (*Author's collection*)

Below: As viewed from the high footbridge close to Langwith Bassett Community Primary School, Brush Type 2 D5827 heads southwards on the Beighton Branch with 1K26 9.38 a.m. Sheffield to Skegness on 11 July 1964. The train has just passed Langwith Junction No. 75 Up Branch Distant signal—in the background can be seen the spoil heaps of Langwith Colliery. Looking at the rusty condition of the rail head in front of the loco, it appears the Up Branch had not been used for a while. No. 1K26 was one of only four passenger services that were running over the Beighton Branch during the summer of 1964. Interestingly, all four workings were unbalanced, that is to say that they would each have different locos working them. In the case of the loco on 1K26, it ran as follows: 9.38 a.m. Saturdays Only from Sheffield Victoria to Skegness, with two stops at Shirebrook North (10.20–10.22 a.m.) and Lincoln Central (11.16–11.22 a.m.), before arriving at Skegness at 12.53 p.m. The return working was 1G15 2.55 p.m. Skegness to Sheffield Victoria, which returned via Gainsborough and Worksop. The remains of the concrete Permanent Way staff cabin adjacent to the train are still to be found today, if you fight your way through the rampant undergrowth. (*J. S. Gilks/Author's collection*)

Gresley K2 2-6-0 61763 approaches the deep cutting with an Up coal train on 13 May 1950. Built by the North British Locomotive Company in Glasgow, Works Number 21984, it was introduced to service in June 1918 as GNR No. 1673, allocated to Doncaster. Becoming LNER 4673 in December 1924, it was renumbered 1763 in 1946, gaining its BR number on 22 January 1949. Its days ended at 34E New England on 6 February 1961, being scrapped that year. (*R. J. Buckley/Author's collection*)

Following the Up Goods train came this triple headed trip from Creswell Colliery, which also approaches the deep cutting on 13 May 1950. Gresley 02 2-8-0 63985 leads Q1/1 0-8-0T 69928 and Robinson 04 2-8-0 63837 on what looks like a brake van and coaches. This might be the breakdown train returning from Creswell Colliery to Langwith Junction after dealing with a derailment. (*R. J. Buckley/Author's collection*)

K3 4-6-0 61908 works the 9.35 a.m. Clowne South to Skegness special on 31 July 1960. This loco was put into service during April 1931, was withdrawn on 19 January 1962, and was scrapped sometime during 1962. (*R. J. Buckley/Author's collection*)

Langwith Colliery Junction

The first branch built along this section was by the Sheepbridge Company, who sunk Langwith Colliery, which commenced in 1876 and was operational from 1880. By the 1870s, The Sheepbridge Coal and Iron Company of Chesterfield already had four collieries in operation, and an upturn in the demand for local coal led the Company to sink Langwith and Glapwell Collieries between 1887 and 1880. Referred to as the 'jewel in the crown' for the Sheepbridge Company, rights to work coal were purchased to the west of Whaley village, from the Earl of Bathurst. Costing £46,000 to develop, it was capable of producing 500 tons of coal per week initially.

Sinking commenced of the 14-foot-diameter No. 1 shaft in March 1876 and reached the 5-foot-10-inch-thick Top Hard seam at 565 yards on 9 February 1878. No. 2 shaft reached the Top Hard on 1 June 1878 at a depth of 538 yards. By 1896, under the management of John Bennett, 1,044 men were employed underground working the Top Hard seam, with 240 on the surface. On Tuesday 18 December 1921, 2,476 tons of coal was turned in two seven-hour shifts. This was a record output for the colliery at the time, and possibly a record for the Nottinghamshire/Derbyshire Coalfield.

Modernisation started in the 1950s, with coal faces being mechanised, and Langwith became the first colliery in the country to operate a rapid loading bunker that could load a full train of coal in around twenty minutes. Coal production ceased on 4 August 1978 and salvage continued until 1979, but the shafts were kept pumping to prevent Creswell Colliery from flooding.

Access to the branch was signalled by Langwith Colliery Junction signal box, which would close on 8 September 1969, access then being from the former MR side only.

Creswell and Welbeck

About a mile further, a branch was built to Creswell Colliery, where shafts of a depth of 445.5 yards were sunk to the Top Hard seam between 1894–6, with production commencing in 1897. In the early years of the twentieth century, the colliery was able to produce an average of between 3,000 and 3,200 tons of coal per day, in this time period holding a world record for winding 3,800 tons in a single day. Production turned to the High Hazels seam in 1942 until it too was exhausted in 1969. After this, the Clowne seam was worked between 1958 and 1968, along with the Three-Quarter seam and Deep Soft seam. By 1949, with a weekly output of about 14,000 tons, it was regarded as one of the most efficient pits in the East Midlands Division. Closure came in September 1991.

Just beyond the junction for the colliery came Creswell Station, which opened on 1 June 1897. Renamed Creswell for Welbeck from 1 September 1897 and later Creswell and Welbeck, it was known locally as 'Top Station' to distinguish it from 'Bottom Station'—the MR Elmton and Creswell station further down Elmton Road. The August 1939 Bradshaw continued to list the station as Cresswell and Welbeck (note use of two 's's).

Markland Grips

Beyond Creswell, the line turned west and crossed the six-arch Markland Grips Viaduct. The 'Grips', as they are known locally, are a network of valleys bounded by cliffs near to the village of Clowne in Derbyshire; in the cliff sides are several fissures and small caves. The viaduct would be affected by subsidence in its later years and would require stabilisation of the arches by wooden beams. However, it would eventually be in-filled to form an embankment.

Clowne

The LD&ECR line almost paralleled the MR Elmton and Creswell to Seymour Junction line to Clowne where the two stations were side by side. The LD&ECR station was spelt Clowne while the MR station was spelt Clown without the 'e'. Both were renamed several times over the years, the LD&ECR one being renamed Clowne and Barlborough from 2 May 1938 and renamed again in 1951 to Clowne South, while the MR station opened in 1888 as Clown, was renamed Clown and Barlborough in 1938 then Clowne and Barlborough in 1951, before closing in 1954.

Above: No. 9F 2-10-0 92083 heads a Class H loaded steel train towards Langwith Junction. It is passing No. 25 Up Home signal, which was removed when the new chord from the former LD&ECR line to the former Midland line was built. This also saw the removal of other semaphore signals and a new No. 2 Down Home colour light, with a route indicator for the colliery line installed. Notice the 24.5-ton wagons on the colliery line: these were introduced for High Marnham power station traffic. This loco was new to 15A Wellingborough in May 1956, eventually being allocated to Annesley on 9 January 1965, then moving to 6C Birkenhead on 22 May 1965—this image must have been taken between those two dates. It would be withdrawn in February 1967 after a life of just under eleven years, and far from life expired. (*Derek Talbot*)

Below: Another 9F 2-10-0, this time 92102, heading towards Langwith Junction with a Class 'C' fitted van train. Again passing No. 25 Up Home, it has already passed No. 26 distant signal, which was beneath Norwood Crossing's Home signal. The signals protecting Norwood Crossing were slotted with the gates there, the signals being attached by wires to the gates, so when the gates were opened to road traffic the signals were replaced to on. As the gates were then closed to road, the signals would again come off. According to relief signalman Gerry Parker, an old hand who worked the crossing, opening the gates to road traffic was a doddle, as the signal weights helped you. Closing them was another matter—you not only had the weight of the gates, but you also had the weight of having to clear the signals as you pushed. The new chord to the Midland side would be built across the field to the right of the loco, notice the neatly kept corrugated iron lamp cabin. (*Derek Talbot*)

Yet another 9F is seen passing No. 25 Up Home: this one is 92200. New to 36A Doncaster on 30 November 1958, it would come to Langwith Junction on 19 June 1965, being condemned from there in October 1965 and cut up at T. W. Wards of Killamarsh, a stone's throw from the Beighton Branch. The loco is working a Class 'C' mixed goods, with several oil tanks at the head. Maybe these are bound for Tuxford or Warsop oil terminals. (*Derek Talbot*)

Seen from Langwith Colliery Junction box, Brush Type 4 D1558 is working 7N79 steel train towards Beighton. The colliery lines lead off left; these closed on 8 September 1969, and access to the colliery was then from the Midland side. No. 7N79 ran the 2.23 p.m. empties from Woodford to Tees Yard, passing Langwith Junction at 5.36 p.m. on Monday–Friday, while on a Saturday ,it left Woodford at 12.50 p.m., but did not pass Langwith Junction until 5.05 p.m. Although undated, this is most probably a 1964 shot, the loco being new to Darnall on 26 February 1964. It would be renumbered 47442 and eventually condemned on 12 March 1993. (*Derek Talbot*)

Above: English Electric Type 3 D6742 on 7M49 1 p.m. Whitemoor to Mottram that ran via Lincoln, Pyewipe Junction, Langwith Junction, Clowne South, and Killamarsh Junction, then via Beighton and Woodhouse to Rotherwood Sidings, where the traction would be changed for an EM1 electric loco through Sheffield Victoria and over Woodhead. Its timings were:

Langwith Junction: 4.18 p.m.
Clowne South: 4.40 p.m.
Spink Hill: 4.47 p.m.
Killamarsh Junction: 4.59 p.m.
Woodhouse East Junction 5.05 p.m.
Rotherwood 5.10 p.m.

The loco was built in 1962, works number EE/VF 3034/D696, and entered service in June 1962, when it was allocated to Darnall. During a nomadic life, the loco was allocated to Cardiff Canton, March, Healey Mills, Thornaby, Tinsley, and Immingham. On the introduction of TOPS, it was renumbered 37042. Although primarily a freight locomotive, D6742/37042 made regular appearances on passenger trains, something which continued until 2004 when it spent two days on Arriva Trains' Leeds–Carlisle loco hauled services with 37411. On the break-up of British Rail, 37042 passed to EWS. It was transferred to the reserve fleet in 2004 before being put into storage in 2007, and finally being sold for preservation in early 2011. No. 37042 arrived at Warcop in April 2011, where it is awaiting restoration. (*Derek Talbot*)

Below: Class 04/8 2-8-0 63612 on an up freight between Creswell Colliery Junction and Langwith Junction on 22 October 1962. The train has just passed Norwood Crossing and has just crossed the A632 road bridge. The houses on the right are Dale Close in Nether Langwith, with Creswell Colliery spoil heaps in the distance, and the chimney belongs to Langwith Colliery. No photos have yet surfaced of Creswell Colliery Junction box, which had an RSCo. thirty-six-lever frame and closed on 8 January 1967.

As for the loco, this was designed by Robinson and introduced to service as GCR 387 in January 1914, it became LNER class 04/1 5387 in November 1925, and received its BR number in September 1950. Rebuilt to 04/8 in July 1955, it was a 41H Staveley allocated loco at the time of the photo, being re-allocated to 41J Langwith Junction from 13 June 1965 and withdrawn in November 1965. (*R. J. Buckley/Author's collection*)

A view of the 'Top Bridge' over Elmton Road in Creswell. The large building on the left is the stationmaster's house, the station itself being situated to the right of the bridge. The bridge was demolished in 1974, but the house still remains today. (*Author's collection*)

The station staff pose for the obligatory photo shoot on the wooden platforms of Creswell and Welbeck station in this undated shot. Opened in March 1897 and closed to passengers in 1939, the station remained open for goods traffic for a while longer. C. W. Gerradine was the stationmaster in 1934, but the 1939 staff returns showed that there was a vacancy for his position and that Wilfred George Padmore was a temporary porter signalman Class 6. Creswell and Welbeck Station signal box had an RSCo. twenty-eight-lever frame, and was abolished along with the closed station on 4 April 1950. (*Kev Birkinshaw collection*)

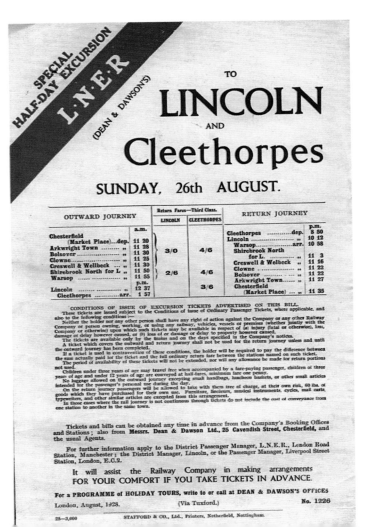

Another group shot on the station, this time the station name is revealed on the bench, comprising metal letters screwed on to the back of the bench. (*Kev Birkinshaw collection*)

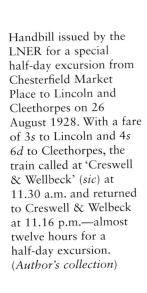

Handbill issued by the LNER for a special half-day excursion from Chesterfield Market Place to Lincoln and Cleethorpes on 26 August 1928. With a fare of 3s to Lincoln and 4s 6d to Cleethorpes, the train called at 'Creswell & Wellbeck' (*sic*) at 11.30 a.m. and returned to Creswell & Welbeck at 11.16 p.m.—almost twelve hours for a half-day excursion. (*Author's collection*)

This photo was taken when the six-arch Markland Grips viaduct was almost newly built and before subsidence set in underneath it. A motley collection of kids are observing the photographer in this postcard image that is dated 1924, but, judging by the condition of the stonework, it is probably from much earlier. (*Author's collection*)

Another view of the viaduct showing that by the early 1920s, the arches had been reinforced due to the subsidence problems that beset the viaduct. Here, a local man and his dog pose for a photo in front of the viaduct. (*Author's collection*)

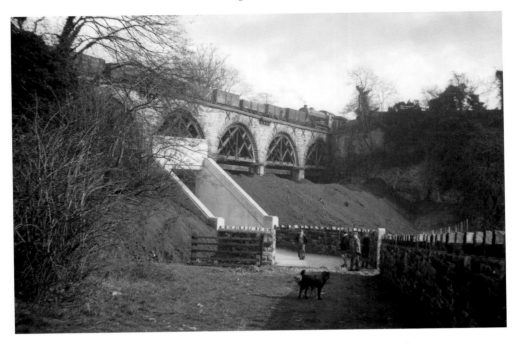

Another motley collection of kids observe the photographer. We can see that a new concrete underpass has been built and the viaduct is being turned into an embankment by infilling. An unidentified LNER 0-6-0 is at the head of a rake of wooden wagons that are in the process of tipping spoil off the viaduct to form the embankment. After closure of the line by BR, the land was sold to an individual who used the route to access the viaduct with large lorries in order to remove materials from the viaduct; these operations ceased in about 1973. The concrete underpass remains today. (*Author's collection*)

Clowne LD&ECR station from a postcard dated 1905—notice the GNR-style somersault signal in the left foreground and that the goods shed and platform buildings on the Down side are combined. The line on the right of the image is the Midland Railway Loading Dock, with the goods office adjacent. (*Derek Talbot collection*)

A platelayer walks through Clowne LD&ECR Station with his long-handled hammer over his shoulder in this shot from a postcard that is dated 1918. (*Author's collection*)

WD 2-8-0 90401, on a train of empty steel wagons, passes through Clowne station on 18 June 1955. Latterly a Langwith Junction engine, it would be condemned on 30 November 1965 and be disposed of at Drapers of Hull in March 1966. (*H. B. Priestley/Author's collection*)

Once fitted on the station building above the tunnel mouth, remarkably the station clock still survives, albeit attached to the former Midland Railway stationmaster's house! (*Author's collection*)

The Railway Signal Company signal box at Clowne Station. Fitted with an RSCo. twenty-nine-lever frame, the box opened in 1895 and is seen here with a complement of staff from the station, along with a couple of bystanders and dog! The child on the balcony appears to be wearing a tri-corn hat. In October 1939, the box was a Class 5 and was staffed by Thomas Edward Kitson, Thomas Bateman and George Ernest Knight, all signalmen Class 5. The box closed on 8 January 1967. (*Glynn Waite collection*)

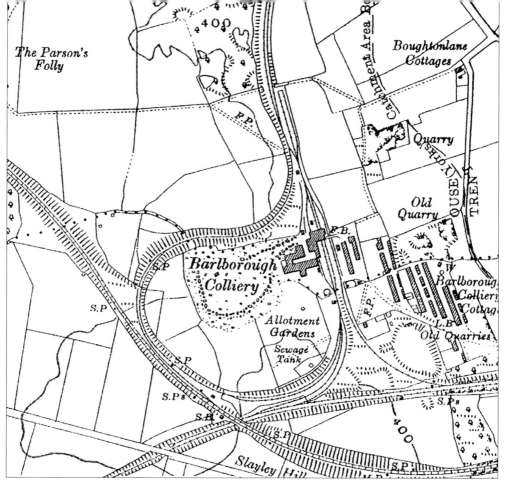

Above: Langwith Junction to Barlborough Colliery Junction was opened for goods and coal trains on 16 November 1896, along with the colliery branches at Barlborough, Creswell, Langwith and Warsop. This map shows the layout at Barlborough and, towards the bottom, where it crossed the Midland Railway's Clowne Branch. (*Author's collection*)

Below: This image, dated 7 June 1934, shows the LD&ECR bridge over the MR Clowne Branch and a signal box. This was originally named Barlborough Colliery Junction but was renamed Oxcroft Colliery No. 3 in 1930, and was abolished on 5 April 1950. This box controlled access to Barlborough Colliery. (*Alan Rowles collection*)

Also close by the station was Southgate (or Clowne) colliery. This colliery was sunk by the Shireoaks Colliery Company and was situated on the Southgate estate at Clowne. Sinking began in 1877, and the Top Hard seam was reached at 321 yards in March 1877 with the initial capacity for 120,000 tons annually. The shaft was 1,000 feet deep by 1900. The LD&ECR colliery sidings were brought into use on 10 May 1896 and, as the colliery was also served by the MR from their Creswell to Seymour line, a connection between the two lines was brought into use on 16 November 1896. On 17 January 1929, a massive in-rush of water from the temporarily abandoned Oxcroft Colliery finally forced the closure of Southgate. The connecting line was closed on 25 April 1937; in 1955, a scheme to re-open Southgate and connect with Creswell colliery workings was started, but was never completed and the shafts were filled in 1961. Today, the site of the colliery is the Station Road Industrial Estate— where an old engine/power house from the colliery still remains in situ.

Leaving Clowne, the LD&ECR bridged the MR Creswell to Seymour Junction line and headed north-west to Barlborough, where two half-mile-long single-line branches were built to serve the colliery, one to the loaded sidings and the other to the empty sidings. The railway connection was controlled by Barlborough Colliery Junction signal box, which was renamed Oxcroft Colliery No. 3 in 1930 before being abolished on 5 April 1950.

Mining in the Barlborough Area

Barlborough has a remarkable history of coal mining, dating back to at least to the sixteenth century. It was a local industry that saw transition from pits that were little more than holes in the ground to more 'modern' deep mines that worked at least seven coal seams. Initially the pits catered for local use, but as markets and transport expanded, so did the investment in technology and deeper large-scale extraction.

The main early beneficiaries were the local land-owning families—the De Rodes, the Poles, and the Bowdens all became rich from coal revenues. Later the larger companies moved in: JG Wells, who owned several collieries in the Renishaw and Eckington areas, and the Appleby-Walker Company of Renishaw Ironworks became involved with the Cottam Collieries (not to be confused with the much later power station of the same name 25 miles further east in Notts); while the giant Staveley Company sank deep, high-capacity collieries in the area as part of their wider coal, iron and steel empire.

It is also likely that the extended demand for coal, together with new markets, opened up by the advent of high-capacity railways, led experienced labour to be drawn away from the small mines to work the larger and deeper high-production collieries in the Barlborough area.

In 1871, the Staveley Company sank Barlborough No. 1 Colliery on the 'Slayleys' area of Barlborough to a depth of 1,603 feet to get to the 64-inch-thick Deep Hard seam, which was used mainly for iron production at the company's works. By 1878, the complex was complete with railway sidings, washery and brick works. The colliery was purchased in 1930 by the Oxcroft Coal Company Ltd (formed in 1901 and a part of the Staveley Company 'Empire') to develop the High Hazel seam. Barlborough No. 1 now became known as Oxcroft No. 3 and continued working until 1946, when severe geological conditions and water problems severely affected production. Fortunately a new face was developed, which allowed the colliery to work until closure in 1949.

There were plans to sink drifts from the surface at the Oxcroft workings down to the Oxcroft No. 3 workings in order to extend the working life of the No. 3 colliery, but, although work commenced in 1938, it was suspended at the outbreak of the war. The drifts were completed by 1944, linking the Oxcroft No. 1 and No. 3 Collieries together. In 1949, the winding of coal out of the Oxcroft No. 3 (formerly Barlborough No. 1) site ceased and instead was brought to the surface via Oxcroft No. 5 drift and washed on the reconditioned plant of Oxcroft No. 1, with men and materials also using this new route. So, while surface plants and shafts had closed at the former Barlborough No. 1, its coal take was still being worked there well beyond 1949. Oxcroft Colliery itself closed in 1974 and the men were transferred to Markham and other local collieries.

The Staveley Company, wanting to enlarge its 'take' in the Barlborough area, had also opened a single shaft mine on Coltsworth Lane at Barlborough in 1896. This colliery, named Barlborough No. 2, was initially sunk to a depth of 687 feet to reach the Top Hard seam. An underground drift connection with Barlborough No.1 completed the ventilation; this route was also used for transportation of coal, via tubs pulled by ponies. Coal never surfaced at No. 2 Colliery. It did not have coal-washing facilities and only men and materials used this shaft—the colliery instead worked the Two Foot, Top Hard, and High Hazel seams, all by hand-got methods. The shaft was deepened in 1925 to a total depth of 1,237 feet to the Deep Soft and Sitwell seams,

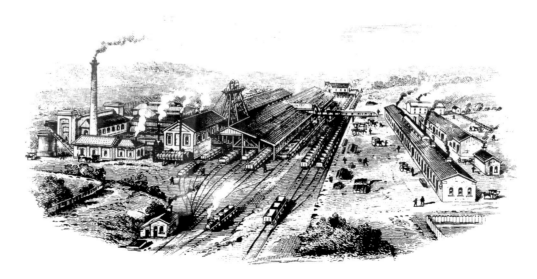

A contemporary print of Barlborough No. 1 Colliery as viewed north in June 1895. Comparing this image with maps, the artist has captured this pretty accurately. The train at the bottom of the image would have been taking the lines towards the LD&ECR and Midland Railway connections. (*Phil Whitehead collection*)

but the colliery closed in 1928, declared as unprofitable. The shaft remained open, however, for upcast ventilation and emergency access to Barlborough No. 1 Colliery. The No. 2 pit shaft was finally sealed in 1949 during the National Coal Board days, but the site continued to be used by the NCB as a coal stocking site. The trains from Barlborough No. 1 commenced running on 16 November 1896.

Barlborough Common

Once past the colliery, the line entered a deep cutting and passed beneath the A619 road, which was supported on a high three-arch bridge.

After passing Barlborough Common, a short branch was built to sidings for Hazel Colliery and Brickyard. Following closure of an old mine—the Cottam No. 2 colliery in 1892—this site lay dormant for some years, with much of the easily accessible coal in the vicinity already worked out by several older or small collieries. Then, in 1909, a consortium of local businessmen formed a company with the initial intention of re-starting the four brick kilns, originally owned by the Cottam Colliery. It was decided that, rather than buy in fuel, they would sink two new shafts on site to access the High Hazel coal—the upcast shaft was 105 feet deep while the downcast reaching a depth of 150 feet.

A Brush Type 2 is seen hauling a long coal train in the deep cutting on the approach to the A619 Bridge at Barlborough on 19 June 1966. This is a rare photo taken from the A619 Bridge near Slayley Lane in Barlborough; behind the camera, the construction of the M1 Motorway through the area between 1965-1968 would sever the branch. (*Brian Wragg*)

This is the A619 Road bridge at Barlborough viewed from track level looking west in July 1976. The M1 Motorway embankment that crossed the track bed can be seen beyond, and within weeks this area was in-filled with household rubbish and landscaped. The bridge parapets remained in view for a long time afterwards, the coping stones gradually disappearing—no doubt to help with some local building project. (*Alan Rowles*)

A portion of an old tramway, which had previously connected Cottam Colliery to Renishaw Ironworks, was utilised to connect down to a main-line siding of the LD&ECR, presumably to transport both bricks and coal to wider markets. In 1912, the company became known as 'The Hazel Colliery & Brickwork Co. Ltd', under the management of a Mr S. L. Robinson. The colliery workforce in 1913 was thirty-one underground with twenty-two on the surface and a further three men in a separate shallow shaft extracting fire clay. The colliery closed in 1914 for coal production, but continued to produce bricks as the Barlborough Brick Company Limited until closure in 1917.

Spink Hill

Shortly before passing through the 501-yard-long Spink Hill tunnel, there was Park Hall Colliery, where Park Hall Colliery signal box was provided to control a siding that had been agreed in October 1907.

A drift mine was developed nearby by the newly formed 'Park Hall Colliery Company' (later the 'Park Hall and Barlborough Collieries Ltd of Spinkhill') to work the High Hazel seam. The drift was worked by an endless wire rope, which then transferred via a tramway to an LD&ECR exchange siding near the east portal of Spink Hill Tunnel, and also over the tunnel onto Syday Lane for local sale. This was short-lived: the colliery closed by 1908 as it was unprofitable. Emerging from the tunnel into a cutting, after passing beneath a road, the next station was Spink Hill, also referred to as Spink Hill for Mount St Mary, as it also served a college founded in 1842 as 'The College of the Immaculate Conception at Spinkhill' by Fr Randal Lythgoe, the Provincial Superior of the Society of Jesus (better known as the Jesuits). Perhaps a little explanation of the name Spinkhill, or Spink Hill, is relevant here. The LD&ECR and its successors always referred to Spinkhill station, tunnel and signal box as 'Spink Hill', though the village name used the spelling 'Spinkhill', which is now universal.

Brickworks at Spinkhill, alongside the branch immediately north of Spink Hill station, were in use in 1920, and in 1923, local mining company J. and G. Wells Ltd sank a single shaft for Westthorpe Colliery, which was to be the final colliery served by the line. Production started in 1928 from the Deep Soft seam at 450 feet and for the next twenty-three years the pit won its entire output from that seam only. Between 1923 and 1947, Westthorpe had three different owners: from 1941 it was taken over by the Tinsley Park Colliery Company, who passed it to United Steel Companies Ltd three years later. In 1949, work started on two drifts at gradients of 1-in-4.5 from the Deep Soft pit bottom into the Parkgate and Thorncliffe seams. From 1951, despite geological problems in the Parkgate, output from these seams and the Deep Soft continued until 1971, after which drifts accessed the Chavery seam to leave that seam as Westthorpe's only production seam for the remainder of its life. Unfortunately, the quality of the Chavery was never the same as that of the earlier seams, and this was a factor which weighed heavily on the eventual closure decision, which happened on 31 March 1984.

A driver's eye view looking towards the north portal of Spink Hill Tunnel in 1977. Buffer stops have been erected just before the tunnel mouth, and the track is used as a shunt neck for Westthorpe Colliery. (*Roger Wainwright*)

A lone gent waits at Spink Hill Station in this very early view that, judging from the condition of the rail head, could be before opening of the line through Spinkhill on 21 September 1898. The station nameboard actually reads 'Spink Hill for Mount St Mary's', a local college. Notice the GNR style somersault signals, which were a feature of the railway. Edwin John Lane, who joined the company on 22 September 1913, held the position of stationmaster here on 31 October 1939, on a salary of £200 per annum. (*Author's collection*)

The Railway Signal Company built Spink Hill signal box; it opened on 16 August 1898 and had an RSCo. twenty-nine-lever frame. It is seen here in 1924, with a proud LNER signalman posing on the steps. Note Westthorpe Colliery on the right. The 1939 staff returns showed that the box was manned by Harry Headley, Class 5 signalman, and Raymond Percival Gamble, porter signalman. The signal box closed on 3 August 1968. (*John Cole collection*)

The driver of 04 2-8-0 63667 looks towards the tunnel at Spink Hill, as he prepares to run round his train via the main-to-main crossover at Spink Hill Station on 8 October 1955. Built by Kitson and introduced to service as WD1629 in September 1918, it became LNER 6367 in 1924 and 63667 in 1950. Allocated to 40E Langwith Junction from 22 September 1951 (code later changed to 41J), it was withdrawn in January 1959. The wooden-bodied former Private Owner 13-ton wagon is number P41008 and still bears traces of its original owner's name. The station looks well looked after, even though it closed to passengers in 1939: the booking office and general waiting room sign is still hanging under the awning. The line of white washing is about to get a covering of smuts from the passing loco! (*Alan Rowles collection*)

Spink Hill in 1977. Westthorpe Colliery internal shunter reposes in the shunt neck, as two rakes of HAA wagons wait in the sidings. This is the view from the cab of a loco as it arrives at Spink Hill with a set of empty wagons. The driver will take the train forward towards the tunnel, before setting back on to the adjacent road. The loco will then be detached and attached to a set of loaded wagons waiting collection, and the internal loco will shunt the empty wagons. Spink Hill station is in the distance, and beyond is the tunnel of the same name. (*Roger Wainwright*)

No. 47319 has drawn towards the tunnel and beneath Station Road Bridge, before setting back with a set of empties for the colliery. These will be loaded to form a train to West Burton or Cottam power station. (*Roger Wainwright*)

Killamarsh

The route continued to curve and, shortly after passing beneath Boiley Lane Bridge, the line then swung almost due-north and began to parallel the GCR main line towards Beighton. On the Down side was a spur into a brickworks, after which was another bridge followed by Killamarsh Station. Renamed Upperthorpe and Killamarsh on the absorption of the LD&ECR by the GCR on 1 January 1907, the station was to close in July 1930, and passenger services over the branch succumbing in 1939.

There were tentative plans to reopen this section of line when the Rother Valley Railway (RVR) was formed on 25 May 1988, and it was originally part of a project known as the 'Friends of Westthorpe', who were based at the old pit complex, along with the Rother Valley Road Transport Group. This project failed to get anywhere and, as such, the RVR decided to go it alone and negotiate with BR for the track to be left *in situ* on the closed line between Beighton Junction and Spinkhill. BR used the northern-most tip at Beighton as a run-round loop, but the society wished to use the remaining line from there as far as Boiley Lane overbridge. This was initially to be the extent of operations, although the track remained in situ past Westthorpe and as far as the tunnel mouth at Spinkhill. They also hoped to be able to build a new station at Rother Valley Country Park to attract custom. Over eighty members purchased the old Signal and Telegraph department (S&T) building from BR at Holmes Junction, to use as a replacement for the long-demolished station buildings at Killamarsh. This portacabin-style building was 40 foot by 16 foot, the same measurements as the original buildings. Several items of rolling

An early view of Killamarsh station sees the stationmaster and his family posing for the camera. Killamarsh became Upperthorpe and Killamarsh on 1 January 1907 to distinguish it from the GCR station at Killamarsh. This is looking south towards Spinkhill, and just beneath the bridge can be seen Killamarsh station signal box. This was another RSCo. box that was shown as 'open as required' by 1925; as such, it was abolished in April 1927. (*Alan Rowles collection*)

No. O4/8 2-8-0 63703 passes the remains of the closed Upperthorpe and Killamarsh Station on a train of hoppers heading for Westthorpe Colliery on 7 June 1960. Built by Robert Stephenson and Hawthorne Ltd in August 1918 and given the WD number 1686, this loco was renumbered 6336 in 1924 and 3703 in 1946, before becoming 63703 in October 1950. It would be withdrawn in January 1965. (*P. H. Robinson/Alan Rowles collection*)

stock were acquired in the form of steam and diesel locomotives, a 5-ton rail crane and it was hoped to acquire a DMU car. The group hoped to reopen the line in July 1990, however, this was not to be and they quietly faded away.

Immediately to the north end of the platforms, the line crossed the Chesterfield Canal, construction of which started in the summer of 1771, and the canal opened throughout from Chesterfield via Staveley, Kiveton, Worksop and Retford to West Stockwith on the River Trent in 1777. This canal, like many others, became a victim of the railway age and, with the opening of the North Midland Railway (a later constituent of the MR) from Derby through Chesterfield to Leeds, and the plans to construct a railway from Sheffield via Worksop to Lincoln, to be known as the Sheffield and Lincoln Junction Railway (S&LJR), the proprietors and shareholders of the Chesterfield Canal were alarmed by the prospect of a railway running parallel to their route through Worksop and Retford and the prospects for loss of long distance and river trade. In response, they promoted their own scheme, the Manchester and Lincoln Union Railway (M&LUR). The S&LJR wisely entered into talks with the M&LUR, and the price of their support was the inclusion of the Chesterfield Canal in the amalgamation. Incorporated on 7 August 1846 as the 'Manchester and Lincoln Union Railway and Chesterfield and Gainsborough Canal Company', the whole awkwardly named undertaking was vested in the new 'Manchester, Sheffield and Lincolnshire Railway' (MS&LR) on 9 July 1847.

After Killamarsh Station, the line rose on a high embankment and crossed Sheffield Road on a steel viaduct, and then crossed the River Rother on a similar viaduct. Between the LD&ECR line and the parallel GCR line was Glovers Flour Mill, and a connection was made from the mill to the LD&ECR line via a steep siding just to the north of the location of the later Killamarsh South Junction.

There were tentative plans by a fledgling railway society called the Rother Valley Railway to reopen the section of line between Upperthorpe and Killamarsh and Westthorpe Colliery, and develop a heritage centre on the site of the colliery. Unfortunately, very little happened and the project eventually disappeared. This is the short-lived Rother Valley Railway base at Upperthorpe, the bridge in the foreground crossing the course of the Chesterfield Canal; notice that the Down line section of bridge has been removed. (*Alan Rowles*)

Looking north towards Beighton, this is Bridge 141 over the Chesterfield Canal on 16 March 1926. Notice again the GNR-style somersault signals and, on the left, the LD&ECR-cast Trespass and Beware of Trains notices. (*Alan Rowles collection*)

The viaduct over today's B6058 at Killamarsh as depicted in the *Engineer Magazine* of 15 December 1899. Although long out of use, the viaduct still stands today. (*Author's collection*)

An unidentified Class 04 2-8-0 brings a rake of hopper wagons laden with coke down towards the River Rother viaduct at Killamarsh; the GCR main line can be seen just below the LD&ECR embankment. The train is approaching Killamarsh South Junction, where the connection between the GCR line and the LD&ECR line is made. (*Alan Rowles collection*)

Class 04/6 2-8-0 63912 of Darnall climbs from Beighton Sidings towards Killamarsh with a lengthy permanent way train on 12 January 1955; the train will soon pass Killamarsh South Junction. Notice the line to Glovers Flour Mill on the left at a lower level. (*Bernard Mettam/ Alan Rowles collection*)

Killamarsh Junctions

With the impending takeover of the LD&ECR by the GCR on 1 January 1907, powers were obtained in the Act of 20 July 1906 to build a new link between the GCR main line and the LD&ECR line at Killamarsh. This steeply graded connection was ready by 1 October 1906, but did not come into use until 25 February 1907. New signal boxes were provided to signal the connection at Killamarsh South Junction on the LD&ECR and Killamarsh North Junction on the GCR main line. Killamarsh South Junction was closed on 24 July 1927 and a new Railway Signal Co. (RSCo.) sixty-lever frame installed in Killamarsh North Junction, which was then renamed Killamarsh Junction.

Beighton Sidings

Moving on past these connections, there was the aforementioned connection to Glovers Mill, then still on its high embankment, the line crossed the MR Killamarsh branch that served Norwood Colliery, and then the GCR Waleswood Curve. This line connected the GCR Main Line to the GCR Sheffield to Worksop line. After crossing over Meadow Gate Lane came connections to sidings on both sides of the line, controlled by Beighton Sidings signal box. Maps show that there were three sidings on the Down side and at least one on the Up side.

Beighton Junction

The end of the branch was reached with the connection to the MR line at Beighton Junction, controlled by Beighton Junction signal box. This was originally planned to be a connection to the MS&LR (later GCR), but Parliament refused to grant running powers over the GCR line from Beighton to Sheffield Victoria via Woodhouse. As such the connection to the MR was made; see later for details of the next part of the LD&ECR route to Sheffield, the Sheffield District Railway (SDR).

Passenger Service

A service of six passenger trains per day between Sheffield and Langwith Junction was inaugurated via the Beighton branch, calling at Attercliffe Road and all intermediate stations on the SDR and LD&ECR. From 2 September 1901, additional stops at Woodhouse Mill and Treeton on the MR were added. A new Mansfield to Sheffield service came in 1903, worked by MR locos and crews, and this replaced the LD&ECR Langwith to Sheffield service. This service ran from Mansfield to Shirebrook and then took the Warsop curve to Warsop Junction, then ran to Warsop before running around and returning via Langwith Junction and the Beighton branch to Sheffield.

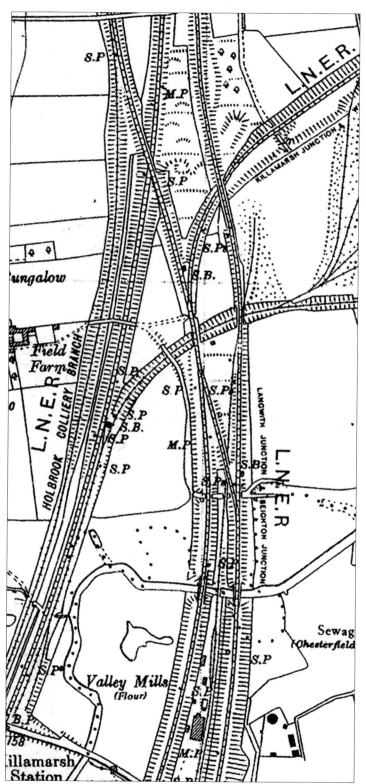

Map of Killamarsh Junctions *c.* 1945. The Midland Railway 'Old Road' comes in bottom left to top, with the LNER Holbrook Colliery branch alongside. The Great Central Main Line from Sheffield to London is centre bottom to top left, crossing over the MR line. The LD&ECR line comes in bottom right with connections to the GCR at Killamarsh Junctions in the centre of the map. Other lines are the MR line to Kiveton going off centre right, with the GCR Waleswood Branch going off top right.

Ex-ROD 2-8-0 63764 brings nearly fifty wagons down the steep 1:82 incline between the former LD&ECR and the GCR main line at Killamarsh. The signal indicates that it will take the Waleswood Curve, which connected with the GCR Sheffield to Worksop line. This loco was built as ROD No 1857 in 1918 and sent over to Europe for the final days of the First World War. Repatriated afterwards and returned to service, it had stints with the Lancashire and Yorkshire and London and North Western Railways. Later stored at Queensferry, it went on to be purchased by the LNER, where it remained in original condition until 1966. The two chaps photographing the movement are Peter Hughes (left) and Bryan Goodlad. (*D. M. Sutcliffe/Alan Rowles collection*)

A3 4-6-2 4472 Flying Scotsman is seen on 18 April 1964 while it works the Great Central Railway Rail Tour. Here it crosses from the GCR to the LD&ECR lines at Killamarsh. Killamarsh Junction box is to the rear of the train, with the semaphore signals for the branch to Waleswood visible. The lines to the right head towards Beighton Sidings and Beighton Junction, while, over to the left, Cow Lane Bridge over the MR line can be discerned. (*Bernard Mettam*)

Above left: The signalman is pictured on the walkway of the LD&ECR Beighton Sidings box, situated some 400 yards south of the junction with the MR. Beighton Sidings box had an RSCo. twenty-four-lever frame and closed on 13 October 1952, but it was not actually demolished until 3 March 1957. (*Brian Newboult collection*)

Above right: Looking north from Beighton Sidings signal box towards Beighton Junction. The sidings are to the right of the photo, just beyond the bridge, which carries a farm track from School Road up the hillside to the left, over the Midland line and GCR mainline, before crossing the LD&ECR. This section of line was in use until 2016 as part of the Westthorpe Run Round Loop. (*Brian Newboult collection*)

Below: This view is almost at the end of the Beighton Branch during the resignalling of the area when it came under Sheffield PSB in 1981. The line from Westthorpe has been singled and is worked under 'One Engine In Steam' regulations: in other words, only one train is allowed between Beighton Junction and Westthorpe at any one time. The signboard to say that this is the end of these regulations is attached to the signal, which now protects the end of the line and the run round loop which has been created. These points would become Sheffield PSB Nos 4169 (*Roger Wainwright*)

Moving on to the next signal, and this is the view of Beighton Junction looking north from the Spinkhill lines towards the junction in 1981. The new Sheffield PSB S281 signal has not yet been commissioned to protect the junction with the Barrow Hill lines. The Old Road from Barrow Hill comes in from the left, while the route to Beighton station and Woodhouse Junction veers off left just beyond Beighton Junction box, which is situated on the right of the picture. (*Roger Wainwright*)

Beighton Junction was the fourth box at this location. Opening on 13 August 1899, it was a MR Type 3b, latterly with a sixty-four-lever LMR Standard 6-inch frame. This view is looking south; the bracket signals protect the main line, while to the centre of the picture the single Home signal, with Distant signal below, protects the end of the former LD&ECR line from Spinkhill. The box closed on 16 May 1982, when the area was taken over by the Beighton Junction interlocking of Sheffield PSB. (*John Midcalf*)

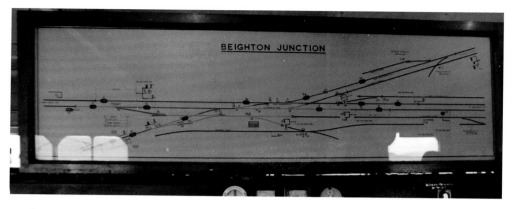

Beighton Junction diagram: the former LD&ECR line towards Spinkhill, by then just single line, can be seen going off bottom left. (*Author's collection*)

This procedure would continue until 1 October 1904, when the MR junctions at Shirebrook Junction opened, thus allowing direct running from Mansfield to Sheffield.

The timetabled passenger service during 1910 was Sheffield to Lincoln and Mansfield (mainly Mansfield, a Midland, and GCR joint arrangement). By 1922, this was down to three trains a day, and the route closed to regular passenger services from 11 September 1939. However, excursions and specials for Mount St Mary College at Spink Hill continued until the early 1960s, and summer Saturday specials to East Coast resorts continued to use the line until 1964.

Closures

Traffic along the Beighton branch typically consisted of coal and through services, usually diversionary or relief traffic off the ex-GCR main line, but with the closure of the GCR line in 1966, much of the diverted traffic disappeared. There were small amounts of other traffic such as the Saturdays Only Wadsley Bridge Bachelor's canning factory to Oddicroft Metal Box factory at Sutton-in-Ashfield, which ran along the Beighton Branch to Langwith then the Leen Valley Extension.

By the 1960s, household coal was in decline and power station coal was on the rise. The construction of West Burton and Cottam power stations in the Trent Valley saw the demand for coal increase and necessitated the introduction of merry-go-round (MGR) working between the collieries in the area and the power stations. The gradients of the route from Shirebrook North to the summit of the Beighton Branch at Clowne and then down to Killamarsh ensured engines had to work hard. The enginemen coined the term 'Clog and Knocker' for the route, as the 1-in-80 and 1-in-100 gradients meant loaded trains would often struggle; with the subsequent increase in MGR train weights, things got no better. Trains off the LD&ECR route would have to traverse the branch to Killamarsh Junction, then along the Waleswood Curve to go east towards Worksop.

With the construction of the M1 Motorway proceeding northwards in the mid-1960s, progress got to a point where it would have crossed the Beighton Branch at Barlborough, thus necessitating a bridge. To avoid the expense of this, the Ministry of Transport paid for the construction of a new double-track chord from the Beighton Branch to the former MR lines just to the north of Langwith Colliery Junction, where the lines ran parallel in the vicinity of Norwood Crossings. Controlled by Langwith Colliery Junction and Langwith Colliery Sidings, its counterpart on the Midland side, this new route opened on 9 January 1967 and allowed trains to travel along the easily graded couple of miles of the Beighton Branch before crossing to the ex-MR line and head for Worksop. Thus, the line northwards from Langwith Colliery Junction to Spink Hill closed to goods traffic from this date.

Buffer stops were erected on the track near the north end of Spink Hill Tunnel, which trains from Westthorpe Colliery used as a shunt neck. Westthorpe's coal then went northwards along the remaining end of the branch, which was renamed the 'Westthorpe Colliery Branch', but the quantities of coal sent out by Westthorpe did not justify the retention of the Waleswood Curve, which thus closed on 9 January 1967. After this, Westthorpe traffic ran to Beighton Junction, then via the former GCR to Woodhouse Junction, where they would have to run round before tackling the 1-in-115 gradient up to Kiveton Park and on to Worksop and the power stations.

Creswell's coal immediately went out exclusively over the ex-MR, and Langwith's followed in 1969. The Oddicroft traffic was diverted to run via Shireoaks, Whitwell—the new MR-LD&ECR spur south of Creswell—through the site of Shirebrook North then onto the Leen Valley extension. Even this ceased with the closure of the Leen Valley Line on 27 May 1968.

By 1974, Bridge No. 37 at Shirebrook North, where the LD&ECR crossed the MR Worksop to Mansfield line, had become weak and was up for renewal. Instead of renewing it, the decision was made to construct a single line chord from the LD&ECR to the former MR close to Warsop Junction and dispense with it completely. This cutting headed south-east, where the closed former MR Welbeck Colliery branch cutting diverged off north-east through the rock cutting, and came into use on 11 November 1974. The remaining section of the Beighton Branch and the chord between the LD&ECR and MR lines at Langwith Colliery Junction were subsequently closed, and all tracks from Shirebrook North onwards thus dispensed with, the track was lifted in the summer of 1976.

As W. H. Davis Wagon Works in the former Langwith Junction Steam Depot area still required access, the 1904 connection from the Down MR line to the Down LD&ECR line was reinstated to provide access to the works. See Chapter Six for further on this.

Trains continued to serve Westthorpe Colliery from the Beighton Junction end; however, this section succumbed after the closure of the colliery in 1984. The final remains of this line at Beighton were a short section used as a run-round loop and reversing siding, still known as the Westthorpe Branch. Latterley this siding was in use for running round coal trains on and off the 'Old Road' and towards Woodhouse Junction; but as coal train lengths became ever longer, it fell out of use, as it could no longer accommodate them. With the downturn in coal traffic, it was taken out of use from 19 September 2016. So ended the last remnants of the Beighton Branch.

View of Langwith Colliery Junction looking north. This is after construction of the new chord across to the former Midland lines. The colliery lines to the right are lifted in this view from 24 January 1971. Langwith Colliery Junction opened on 28 December 1896, with a twenty-five-lever frame that was later extended to twenty-nine. The box originally worked to Langwith Junction and Creswell Colliery Junction. (*Author's collection*)

View from Langwith Colliery Junction box looking north in 1970, with the empty trackbed towards Norwood Crossing, Creswell & Welbeck and Beighton heading off northwards. The double track chord from the Beighton Branch to the Midland line was built to allow loaded trains from the LD&ECR-served collieries to access Cottam and West Burton power stations without traversing the heavy gradients towards Clowne. It was built where the routes ran parallel in the vicinity of Norwood Crossings. Controlled by Langwith Colliery Junction and its counterpart on the Midland side, Langwith Colliery Sidings, this new route opened on 9 January 1967. In this view, the chord towards the former Midland Shirebrook to Creswell route heads off right. (*Derek Talbot*)

This is the Midland end of the chord, looking north towards Norwood Crossing with the crossing keeper's house being prominent. This shot was taken after 11 November 1974, when the chord had closed. Langwith Colliery Junction box had closed in June 1971, after which the Langwith Junction box then worked through to Langwith Colliery Sidings box on the Midland side (behind the camera, to the right). In conjunction with the opening of the new chord at Shirebrook (East) Junction, Langwith Junction box and this chord were subsequently closed and the lever for No. 4 Up Midland to Up GC points (operated by Langwith Colliery Sidings) was then reused as the Down Intermediate Block Home to Elmton and Creswell. (*Derek Talbot*)

The end for the Beighton Branch, as a JCB machine lifts sleepers from the track and places them into the wagons of 9G13, a Class 37 hauled engineers train. This view is looking north towards Langwith Colliery Junction, and beyond the bulldozer Langwith pit tips can be seen. (*Derek Talbot*)

3

The Sheffield District Railway

The Sheffield District Railway (SDR) was conceived as an independent route by which the LD&ECR could reach Sheffield, utilising running powers via the MS&LR line from Beighton into Sheffield Victoria. However, the MS&LR had been one of the opponents to the original LD&ECR Bill and, while their opposition to this new company did not prevent the LD&ECR from obtaining an Act, Parliament did not grant running powers into Sheffield Victoria. Subsequently, four Sheffield businessmen—Sir George Reresby Sitwell, Mr Robert Fenwick Mills, Mr Peverill Turnbull, and Alderman Gainsford—came together to try and garner interest in short connecting lines around the Sheffield area that would be of benefit to both the LD&ECR and the MS&LR. At the time of asking the LD&ECR to take an interest (1894), the company's finances were in a poor state and they were unable to help, while the GER also refused the plea; as a result, the plan went no further.

The same businessmen made another plea in 1896, this time to build an independent route from the LD&ECR at Spink Hill through Hackenthorpe, Handsworth and Darnall, with running powers again for passenger traffic via the MS&LR from a spur at Tinsley to Sheffield Victoria. On 4 August 1896, the SDR was incorporated and, as the LD&ECR still had a desire for its trains to reach Sheffield, was backed by the LD&ECR and eventually the GER. Although the MS&LR would still not grant running powers over their line, the GER and LD&ECR were to enjoy running powers over the SDR line. The LD&ECR agreed to work the line for 50 per cent of gross receipts, but the SDR would remain in charge of maintenance of the permanent way. However, the lack of running powers into Sheffield Victoria had virtually confined the SDR to being a freight-only line: the Attercliffe terminus was well positioned for goods traffic, but too far from the city centre to be of use as a passenger terminal of any significance.

In a competitive blow, the MR also promoted a Bill for a line in the following Parliamentary session. This railway was to be 3.5 miles long, starting from a junction to the north of Sheffield, and travelling between the Rotherham to Sheffield line at Brightside and the MR main line at Treeton. This unexpected move led the SDR to begin urgent talks with the MR, as it was expected that obtaining capital would be very difficult and profits on two competing lines was likely to be very sparse.

There was to be a favourable outcome to the talks, with agreement that the SDR would take over the MR scheme; the revised plan was much shorter than the original plan, which would have been 9.5 miles long. The MR were to grant perpetual running powers to the two companies over the line, and then along the MR line from Brightside into Sheffield, to a point where the spur to the SDR's proposed Attercliffe Goods terminal would be formed, with further running powers for passenger trains to continue into Sheffield Pond Street station.

Harry Willmott, the General Manager of the LD&ECR, liked the new scheme and persuaded his Board to support it, thus clearing the way for a further Bill to be put in front of Parliament. The abbreviated route was sanctioned by Parliament in an Act of 12 August 1898, which incorporated the running powers for the LD&ECR and the GER over the MR, and permitted the MR running powers over the SDR.

Work Begins

Prior to the MR's proposals, construction of the line began on 20 November 1896, when the Duke of Norfolk cut the first sod at Attercliffe. The contractor for the line was Messrs Price and Wills, while a contract for £15,841 was also awarded to Price and Wills to extend the Beighton Branch to connect with the MR at Beighton. This connection was south of the MR/MS&LR junction at Beighton, thus through-running to Sheffield Victoria could still be accomplished if required. The route was opened on 20 May 1900 by the Duke of Portland, which coincided with the opening of the northern section of the Beighton Branch. The opening ceremony included a luncheon

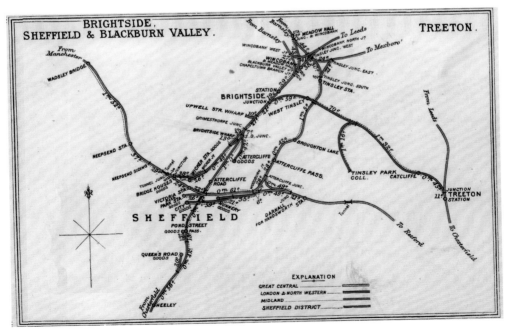

A railway clearing house map showing the Sheffield District Railway in blue, running from the MR (green) at Treeton, through to the MR (also in green) at Brightside. (*Author's collection*)

for 400 guests, among whom were the Lord Mayor of Sheffield, the Duke of Portland, and the GER Chairman, Lord Claud Hamilton. Goods traffic commenced running on 29 May 1900, with passenger traffic the following day. From 28 May 1901, the LD&ECR took over maintenance of the permanent way and works.

The Route Described

Starting from the Treeton end on an embankment, the first engineering feature was the nine-arch Catcliffe viaduct across the Rother Valley. The arch over the Rother itself had a 40-foot span, while the remaining eight spans were 30 foot, one of which was later bricked up and used as business premises, occupied by a Mr J. Russell Boot Repairer, along with a grocer and fruiterer. Stations were of wooden construction due to the nature of their positions on embankments. The first station, at Catcliffe, half a mile from Treeton, was nicknamed 'Klondike' by the locals due to its bleak location. Catcliffe was followed by the 80-yard long Tinsley Wood tunnel near Brinsworth. Beyond the tunnel, the line was still in cutting in open countryside, then, after passing beneath Wood Lane, the line rose on another embankment, and then passed beneath Park House Lane, where a connection was made to a branch to Tinsley Park Colliery in 1903.

The view towards Sheffield from Catcliffe station when it was open to passengers; at least thirteen passengers await a train. Catcliffe signal box is at the end of the platform: it was situated 1135 yards from Treeton Junction and was an RSCo. box with a twenty-nine-lever RSCo. Tappet locked frame that was built in 1900. During 1956, the box was shown as open from 7.45 a.m. to clearance of the last freight train on Monday to Friday, and 7.45 a.m. to 11.35 a.m. on Saturday. Although a definitive date for the closure of the box has not come forward, it was shown in the Sheffield Area freight Working Time Table (WTT) of 10 September 1962 to 16 June 1963, but not in the following WTT, which commenced 17 June 1963 (*Author's collection*)

The wooden platforms of Catcliffe station as viewed towards the nine-arch viaduct and Treeton Junction, this opened with the line in July 1900. Although undated, this photo shows the Up advanced starting signal just beneath the station building canopy at the far end of the platform. As this was moved to this position in May 1911, when a new siding to Hadfield's Works on the Up side of the line at the far end of the viaduct was commissioned, it must date from after that time, and, as the nameboards have been removed, probably after 1939. (*Author's collection*)

The only tunnel on the line was the 80-yard-long Tinsley Wood, and this is the view of the cutting and tunnel looking towards Catcliffe. The large pipe is one of four gas mains belonging to the United Coke and Chemical Company that had to be diverted when Tinsley Marshalling Yard was built. The cutting and tunnel was filled with spoil from the construction of the yard. (*Author's collection*)

Tinsley Park Colliery

The only colliery to be served along the route was Tinsley Park, the history of coal mining in the Tinsley area of Sheffield being somewhat complicated. In the early nineteenth century, the area was a complex of small individual pits spread over an area of about 1 square mile. Earl Fitzwilliam's Estates were responsible for the sinking of a colliery at Tinsley in 1819. However, in 1852 the first deep shaft was sunk by the newly formed Tinsley Park Colliery Co. Ltd. This initially produced about 4,000 tons of steam and house coal a week. Served by a branch over 1 mile in length, further shafts were sunk in June 1902 and 1909, increasing output to 9,000 tons per week and employing a workforce of 2,000.

A Cornish engine house once stood on No. 8 shaft at Tinsley Park, this being purchased second-hand for the price of £1,800 in 1873 and originally built by Copperhouse Foundry, Hayle, Cornwall. An additional sum of £120 was charged for the dismantling and transportation of the engine from Wheal Seton tin mine, near Redruth. This structure was still onsite many years after closure of the colliery, which occurred in early 1943. After closure, the site was used by the Ministry of Fuel and Power as 'West Tinsley Disposal Point' from *c.* 1945 until September 1957, with the track being removed in December 1957.

After passing over Shepcote Lane, the line then crossed the Sheffield and South Yorkshire Navigation canal, followed by the MS&LR Sheffield–Rotherham line on a steel girder bridge. Next came a bridge over Attercliffe Common, and just west of this was Tinsley Road station, 2 miles and 57 chains from Treeton Junction. This station had two wooden platforms, each with wooden buildings, this being to reduce weight as the station was situated on top of an embankment. It was renamed West Tinsley by the GCR from 1 July 1907. There was also a goods warehouse and yard adjacent to West Tinsley Station—being at road level, this was reached by a fairly steep incline. The Edgar Allen and Company's Imperial Steel Works was also reached via this incline.

It was planned that the station be reopened under the South Yorkshire County Council Transport Plan in 1990, where it would serve the Meadowhall Leisure complex to be known as 'Tivoli Gardens' (later 'Bourbon Street'). The station was to have been served by trains on a diverted Sheffield to Lincoln service, which would also call at the planned Swallownest station, and the stations at Darnall and Woodhouse would have closed. However, this idea came to nought, the project never materialised and the Lincoln service remained as it was, with the line from Brightside Junction to Shepcote Lane (the north end of Tinsley yard) being closed and lifted.

The remaining distance connected the SDR to the MR line at Brightside Junction. Engineering features on this section included Brightside viaduct, a seven-span structure with a lattice girder span of 100 foot over the River Don, and an 80-foot plate girder bridge crossing Meadow Hall Road, beyond which the tracks curved south to meet the MR a short distance south of Brightside Station.

Above: Tinsley Park Colliery signal box. The inspection report for this signal box was made on 16 December 1903 for a new sidings layout and a 1-mile-long branch to Tinsley Park Colliery, which had opened on 30 November 1903. The box was 1 mile and 397 yards from Catcliffe and had a thirty-four-lever RSCo. Tappet locked frame. In 1956, the box was shown as open 7.40 a.m. to 3 p.m. on weekdays only. This photo dates from the early 1960s and is before the commencement of works to build the new Tinsley Marshalling Yard. A closure date for the box is not definite, but it was shown in the Sheffield Area freight WTT for 10 September 1962 to 16 June 1963, but was not in the following WTT, commencing 17 June 1963, so its closure date was possibly in late 1962 or early 1963. (*Author's collection*)

Below: Tinsley Park Colliery with several private owner wagons in view. The nearest is a recently painted Tinsley Park Kilnhurst Collieries No. 4297, next to it is Stewarts & Lloyds Kilnhurst Collieries No. 4970, then Stewarts and Lloyds Tubes No. 4420. Tinsley Park Colliery itself closed in 1943. (*Author's collection*)

West Tinsley Station opened on 30 September 1900 as Tinsley Road, but this station was closed just before the outbreak of the Second World War. West Tinsley signal box can be seen beyond the far end of the Up platform, this was 1 mile and 185 yards from Tinsley Park Colliery and was shown as having a fifty-lever RSCo. Tappet locked frame. In the inspection report from 5 July 1900, it was shown as having thirty-six working and fourteen spare levers. In 1956, the opening hours were 6 a.m. Monday to 10 p.m. Saturday; although long closed to passenger traffic, West Tinsley station did not close to public goods traffic until 3 October 1960. The box was shown in the Sheffield Area WTT running from 9 September 1963 to 14 June 1964, as open 6 a.m. to 9.02 p.m. Monday to Friday, and 6 a.m. to 1.50 p.m. on Saturdays.

Although a definitive closure date for the box has not come forward, the March 1963 LMR Midland Lines Supplementary Operating Instructions shows that the Sheffield District line then ran between Tinsley Park Colliery and Brightside Station Junction. Meanwhile, Supplement No. 1 to the Sectional Appendix of 1960, dated March 1964, says that West Tinsley had been abolished and replaced by Shepcote Lane signal box, which was 85 yards further from Brightside. All of this work was in connection with the construction of Tinsley Yard. (*Author's collection*)

Attercliffe Road

The SDR built a large goods depot at Attercliffe, which was temporarily worked by the MR from 20 December 1899. This was accessed from a branch at Sheffield District Junction seven chains south of Grimesthorpe Junction.

There were two girder bridges and a twin span bridge over Sanderson's Mill Race along this short section before Attercliffe Goods Depot was reached, 4 miles and 36 chains from Treeton Junction. The 40-acre goods yard required substantial supplementary works during construction, including a diversion of the River Don and the ground level raising by 12–15 feet. The goods shed building itself was two stories high, with provisions made for possible future extensions. It was provided with hydraulic cranes and a steam-operated overhead crane. Apart from the usual facilities (cattle pens, horse and carriage docks etc.), there was also a platform provided for passengers which, as far as is known, was never used for its intended purpose.

For such a short line, there were a large number of private sidings due to the nature of the heavy industry in Sheffield. Several other short branches opened in 1903 to serve local industries, including Cooper and Co., Hadfield's Steel Foundry, William Jessop and Sons, Sanderson Brothers and Newbould, and Woodhouse and Rixon.

As seen through the window of the Midland Railway Grimesthorpe Junction No. 1 box looking south, a MR train, with what looks like a 0-4-4T loco at the head, shuffles past Grimesthorpe Junction No. 2. On the right of the box, a saddle tank loco shunts the Cyclops Works. The lines swinging in from the left come from the loco depot yards, while the lines beyond the signals that swing left lead to the Sheffield District Railway Attercliffe Goods Depot. (*Author's collection*)

The Goods and Grain Warehouse at Attercliffe as built for the LD&ECR, but by now in GCR ownership. It was classed as second in importance to the GCR Bridgehouses Depot in Sheffield. Attercliffe Goods signal box controlled the confines of Attercliffe Goods Depot and had an RSCo. frame that was reported as having thirty levers in 1933. 1,053 yards from Grimesthorpe Junction No. 1 signal box, the box opening hours in 1956 were 5.30 a.m. Monday to 10.30 p.m. Saturday. (*Author's collection*)

This enamel British Railways sign was still attached to the entrance to the Goods Depot after closure. When the demolition men began to take down the buildings, the former owner of the Cleethorpes Coast Light Railway rescued it and took it to Cleethorpes for display. It is still on display today at the railway's Lakeside station. (*Author's collection*)

Signalling

Traffic on and off the Sheffield District route was controlled by signal boxes at Treeton, (renamed Treeton Junction) on the MR 'Old Road' and Brightside Junction. Signal boxes on the route were provided by the Railway Signal Company (RSCo.) at Catcliffe, Tinsley Park Colliery, and West Tinsley, with RSCo. tappet-locked frames. The signalling lists of 1933 and 1934 give total numbers of levers as twenty-nine for Catcliffe, thirty-four for Tinsley Park Colliery and fifty for West Tinsley, but these totals may not include spaces. Attercliffe Goods signal box controlled the confines of Attercliffe Goods Depot, with a thirty-lever RSCo. tappet-locked frame as noted in 1933. May 1911 saw a new siding to Hadfield's Tip commissioned on the Up side of the line at the Treeton end of the Catcliffe viaduct, with a new ground frame released by Catcliffe signal box.

Traffic Ceases

The SDR closed to passengers from 11 September 1939 for the duration of the Second World War, but reopened briefly afterwards from 6 October 1946 until 17 March 1947. Goods traffic continued afterwards, Catcliffe station closed to public traffic in 1955, but the Hadfield's Tip siding remained in use. The September 1960 traffic notices showed that West Tinsley warehouse traffic had ceased, and that only siding traffic was handled from 3 October 1960.

Tinsley Marshalling Yard

The year 1965 saw a major change to the SDR. When the modernisation of Sheffield's railways was undertaken, it was decided that changes would have to be made to Sheffield's freight traffic, with its multitude of small yards. Consequently, the new Tinsley Marshalling Yard was constructed along the route of the SDR at a cost of £11 million. Massive earthworks were necessary to provide space for the yard, which completely changed the nature of this route. Work started on the new yard in August 1961 and culminated with the opening in 1965. New connections were built at both ends of the route and new signal boxes provided at Brightside Junction and in the yard itself. The location also allowed easy access to the brand-new Tinsley Diesel Depot. The Supplementary Operating Instructions of March 1963 gave notice to delete the line between Treeton and West Tinsley from the Appendix, while the Hadfield's Tip siding at Catcliffe was deleted from the notices by April 1963. However, it has recently been discovered from paperwork salvaged from Tinsley Yard PSB that Hadfield's Tip Siding closed *c.* June 1967, the connection being taken over by Tinsley Yard PSB in 1965.

Tinsley Park signal box was commissioned on 29 November 1964, Shepcote Lane on 7 December 1964 and Tinsley Yard on 11 April 1965, but there was a temporary signal box at Shepcote Lane in use before the new PSB was opened there. No actual closure dates have come forward for the Catcliffe and Tinsley Park signal boxes, but they would have been abolished by the time of the commissioning of the new boxes.

4
LD&ECR Locos, Depots, and Works

LDECR Locomotives

The LD&ECR never had any tender locomotives, and tank locomotives, all built by Kitson and Co., reigned supreme throughout the company's short life. There were just four types used: Class 'A' 0-6-2T, Class 'B' 0-6-0T, Class 'C' 0-4-4T, and the largest Class 'D' 0-6-4T.

Depots and Works

The main locomotive depot and works of the LD&ECR were at Tuxford. However, the company also built a small depot at Langwith Junction to house just two Class 'B' 0-6-0Ts, which were based there to shunt the colliery yards, and there was also a shed at Chesterfield Market Place.

Chesterfield Depot

Chesterfield Depot was situated on a small piece of land between the main line and the MR Brampton Branch, on an embankment to the east of Park Road. It was a two-road affair, able to provide cover for two of the company's tank locomotives, one to shunt the goods yard and the other to work the first morning passenger train out of Chesterfield Station.

No photograph has come to light of the building itself, although an old postcard exists that shows part of the Queen's Park cricket ground and the Pond Houses, taken from the high ground to the south, and gives a distant view of the engine shed.

The building would have a short life, as it was destroyed by fire discovered at five o'clock in the morning of Sunday 19 April 1903 by a watchman named Kilby. Although the Borough Fire Brigade was alerted and a vain attempt made to save the building, due to the fact that water had to be obtained from Park Road, instead of the railway company's water hydrant, which was located in the middle of the blazing shed, it was all to no avail.

The LD&ECR had thirty-seven locomotives divided into four classes, all of which were built by Kitson and Company of Leeds. Eighteen Class 'A' 0-6-2Ts were built between 1895 and 1900 for goods trains. They became LNER class N6 and were withdrawn between 1933 and 1938. Here is No. 7 reposing on Tuxford Depot. (*Author's collection*)

Four Class 'B' 0-6-0T were built in 1897 for shunting, becoming LNER Class J60, and all were withdrawn between 1947 and 1948. This is No. 12 in works photographic grey livery. Nos 9–12 were renumbered 1175–8 by the GCR. Pre-Grouping, the J60s (as they became known) were usually based at Langwith Shed and used for shunting at Warsop sidings, with one often being based at Tuxford for use as the works pilot. By 1923, the Tuxford locomotive had been transferred to Wrexham, and the three others later followed. (*Author's collection*)

Six Class 'C' 0-4-4T were built between 1897 and 1898 for passenger trains. These became LNER class G3 and were withdrawn between 1931 and 1935. Again in works photographic grey livery, this is No. 16. (*Author's collection*)

The largest locos were Class 'D', with nine of these 0-6-4T being built between 1904 and 1906 for coal trains; this is No. 29 in works grey livery. They became LNER class M1 and, with the exception of two brief allocations by No. 6149 to Ardsley (in 1927) and Lincoln (in 1934), the M1s spent their entire working lives working from Langwith and Tuxford. Initially built to haul coal trains to Grimsby, they were quickly displaced by GCR J11 0-6-0s and Q4 0-8-0s when the LD&ECR was absorbed by the GCR. The M1s then moved to a mixture of trip, shunting, and assistance duties. In about 1921, the Langwith M1s were allocated a goods train duty to Woodford and also acted as pilots near Sheffield Victoria, assisting heavy coal trains towards Dunford Bridge. Withdrawals started in 1939, and the last one was withdrawn in 1947. (*Author's collection*).

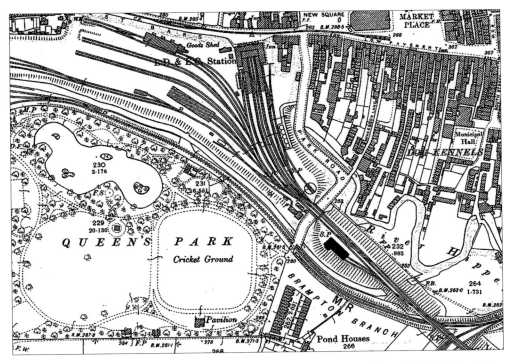

This map of Chesterfield Market Place shows the location of the Chesterfield Market Place shed, picked out in solid black. The depot was shown on maps of 1898, but had gone on the 1918 maps. (*Courtesy Network Rail Corporate Archive*)

Inside the shed, a wagon full of coal was completely consumed, while a visiting contractor's engine that belonged to Messrs Brown & Howie, along with LD&ECR Class 'C' 0-4-4T locomotive No. 16, sustained considerable damage. Fortunately, the General Manager had insured the building with the Royal Insurance Company under Policy Number 7481741, and had paid the current annual premium of seventeen shillings and sixpence, which enabled a claim for £500 to be submitted. However, the LD&ECR only received a payment of £350 relating to the damage caused to its own locomotive and building.

By referring to the original insurance policy, some idea of the construction of the shed building can be obtained. The main building was 150 feet 8 inches long by 36 feet 6 inches wide, and is described as a 'locomotive shed', having steel domes or sheet iron smoke troughs and chimneys in the roof and furnished with two fitters benches. There was a men's mess room that contained a closed fire cooking stove in the centre, which stood on legs 6 inches high in a thick cast iron pan resting on a wooden floor. The chimney piping was fitted with a vertical sheet iron flue through the roof, passing through an outer iron pipe with air space between, and the floor around the stove was covered with lead. The remaining two rooms are described simply as an office and conveniences. It was a single storey timber-built building with a felt roof that, according to the local newspaper report, had recently been tarred. Lighting for the whole building was by gas. The building would not be rebuilt, but No. 16 was returned to service.

Above: Looking across Queens Park to the railway, we can see the bridge over Park Road and the Water Tower dead centre with the signal box behind it, while over to the right we can see a row of houses on Park Road. The most interesting part of the photo though is what is behind the houses: could that roof with the vents be the engine shed. If it is, then the roof is different to the one in the plan, which was a 'north light' style—the diagram and photo leave us with many questions. (*Author's collection*)

Below: Although no photographs have surfaced of Chesterfield Market Place depot, this diagram of the shed has remarkably survived and is in the Network Rail Archive. It shows it was a two-road building 150 foot and 8 inches long by 36 foot and 6 inches, with latrines, store room and mess room in a lean-to annex. (*Courtesy Network Rail Corporate Archive*)

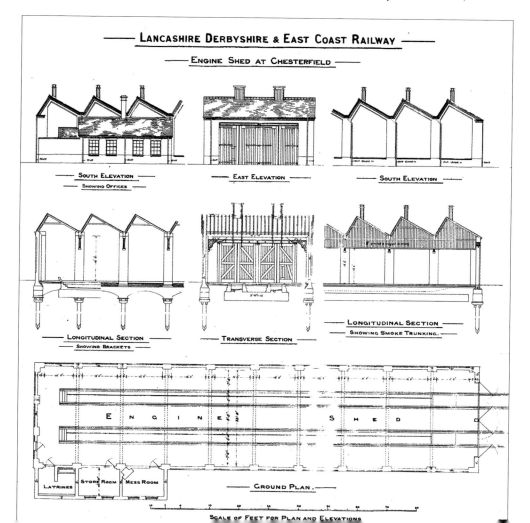

Tuxford Depot and Wagon Works

Tuxford Shed was situated on the north side of the line, within the triangle of the connecting chord to the GNR and the main line (see Volume Two). It was a three-road shed, with one being a through road. The shed was equipped with a water softening plant, but there was no turntable. Coaling facilities were crude to say the least, right until the end. Originally expected to be the main LD&ECR depot, it was soon realised that the main centre of activity would be Langwith Junction.

At Grouping on 1 January 1923, there were eight Class 'D' 0-6-4T (LNER Class M1) locos allocated to Tuxford. These were used for trip, shunting and banking duties, along with eight Class 'A' 0-6-2T (LNER Class N6) for trips and shunting.

By 1950, Tuxford had an allocation of seven Class 04 2-8-0s and eight Class J11 0-6-0s, but it closed as a steam depot on 2 February 1959. Its allocation of twelve Class 04 2-8-0s and five Class J11 0-6-0s moved to Langwith along with the men, a daily 'DIDO' (Day In-Day Out) train being provided for the staff concerned. The building would remain open for wagon repairs afterwards.

The loco and wagon works, known locally as 'The Plant', was situated outside the curve to the GNR on the northern side of the LD&ECR. It was small but capable of replacing loco boilers and fireboxes, and employed 130 men. The works office was built in a similar style to that of the station buildings along the route, and was home to

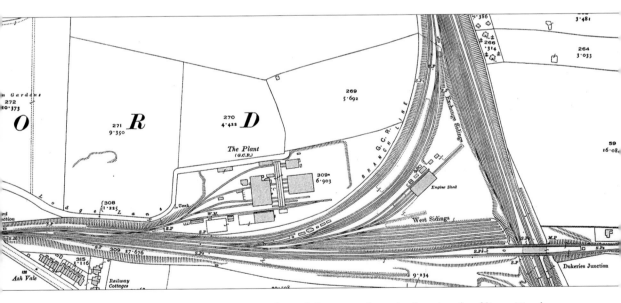

The Tuxford area, showing the wagon works and the steam depot in the triangle of lines. North to south is the GNR main line, with Dukeries Junction to the bottom. Opened on 16 November 1896, the first Tuxford depot was a two-track affair, built of brick and open at both ends, with facilities including a coaling stage and a water tank. Expansion of the building turned it into a three road straight through shed with a transverse multi-pitched slate roof. Given the code 40D from 1 February 1950, it became 41K from 1 July 1958, before closing on 2 February 1959.

Here is former LD&ECR No. 32 on shed at Tuxford. This became GCR 1151, then LNER 6151 from February 1924, and was renumbered 9082 in May 1946. It would be withdrawn in July 1947. (*Author's collection*)

Tuxford shed during a rainy day in July 1930 sees a selection of motive power on shed. From left to right, J11 0-6-0 5300, an N6 0-6-2T (formerly LD&ECR Class 'A'), M1 0-6-4T 6145 (formerly Class 'D') and an unidentified O4 2-8-0. The M1 would be withdrawn in September 1941, but its chassis would be used as a boiler carrier at Gorton Works until November 1955. (*Author's collection*)

J11 5214 on the coal stage at Tuxford on 8 May 1946, not long before it was renumbered 4337. It would then become BR 64337 and survive until June 1961, being withdrawn from 9G Gorton. (*Author's collection*)

Another J11, this time 5982 is seen at the west end of Tuxford shed on 8 May 1946. This loco would be renumbered to 4289 then BR 64289, being withdrawn from Langwith Junction in 1955. (*H. C. Casserley/Author's collection*)

A former LD&ECR six-wheel brake third-class coach sits on the traverser at Tuxford Works in July 1930. It is now numbered as LNER 51838. (*Author's collection*)

Tuxford Works in GCR days, with a good selection of wagons on show. (*Author's collection*)

the Chief Mechanical Engineers of the line and various office staff. To lift large parts, a set of 'sheer legs' was installed in front of the main building.

Closed by the LNER as a locomotive works in 1927, it continued as a carriage and predominantly wagon works for many years thereafter. The buildings remained more or less intact after closure, but by 1977 all the ancillary buildings were demolished, leaving the main erecting halls. These are still used today as part of Lodge Lane Industrial Estate.

Langwith Junction Depot

The original shed at Langwith was on the south side of the line, a few yards from the ends of the platforms of Langwith Junction station. With the increasing importance of coal traffic, it was realised that a larger depot was needed at Langwith, and a two-road brick shed was built, large enough to house up to fourteen tank locos. Later on, a three-road straight carriage shed was to be added which survived until the end, albeit only used to store the breakdown train and locos under repair in its latter days. In 1935, the original inclined-ramp coaling stage was replaced by a new concrete Mitchell coaling plant, and a new larger turntable was installed in 1945. In the 1940s, the LNER proposed a new depot that would be built in the triangle of land formed by the LD&ECR main line, the Warsop Curve and the Midland line. Although the proposals went as far as a plan to show the possible layout of a six-road straight shed and how it could be affected by mining subsidence, nothing else came of it.

Langwith Junction was to be the base of a wide variety of locomotives for working the passenger and freight services. These would vary in size, from the diminutive class 'B' 0-6-0 tanks of the LD&ECR, to the giants that were the BR's 9F 2-10-0s. Although coal was to be the main source of traffic, the Langwith Junction men also worked the passenger services on the LD&ECR line from Chesterfield to Lincoln and Sheffield.

For shunting the yards, N5 0-6-2Ts replaced the J60 and N6 tanks, whilst 04 2-8-0s were utilised on the longer freight turns and J11 and Q1 locos for trip working. On the passenger side, a batch of GNR C12 4-4-2Ts worked the remaining Chesterfield–Lincoln passenger service.

October 1947 saw most of the 04s replaced with Gresley 02 2-8-0s until 1950, when they were moved away again, being replaced by the 04s. After trials with 0-6-2T classes N2, N7, and an LMS 'Tilbury Tank', the C12s were finally replaced. Although the 0-6-2Ts ran well enough, after a derailment or two due to track holding and the like, three A5 4-6-2Ts were drafted in. They were most welcome at Langwith.

The last day of the LNER, 31 December 1947, saw the following locomotives allocated to Langwith Junction:

Q4 0-8-0T	3227
04 2-8-0	3597/644/65/77/837
O2 2-8-0	3921/23/24/25/26/27/28/42/43/45/46/65/66/67/68/69/70
	3971/72/73/74/79/80/81/82/83/84/85/86/87
J11 0-6-0	4281/89/97/321/33/58/78/79/89/414/18/26/27/50

Former LD&ECR Class 'A', now GCR N6 0-6-2T 1162, is seen in its GCR livery at Langwith. Withdrawn from Langwith in October 1935, it would be cut up the following month at Doncaster. (*Author's collection*)

Still in its LNER livery, Parker N5 0-6-2T 9323 gets a little oiling round at Langwith on 10 July 1949. Introduced in 1900 by the Manchester Sheffield & Lincolnshire Railway (MS&LR, later GCR) as the N4, it would become BR 69323 and end its days at 39B Darnall on 30 November 1956. (*B. K. B. Green/Author's collection*)

Twenty-five of the Langwith Shed staff pose with an unidentified Class 04 2-8-0, sometime between 1923 and 1929. (*Author's collection*)

Great Northern Railway 4-4-0s had been seen regularly on depot during the war years, but by the time Boston-allocated D2 2181 came to spend the weekend at Langwith on 26 March 1950, they were very rare birds. Indeed, this was probably the last time one visited, as they had all gone by 1951; this one was allocated BR number 62181 but only lasted in service until November 1950, so it is unlikely it ever received the number. (*Lawson Little*)

Gresley Class 02/3 2-8-0 receives attention to one of its cylinders at Langwith. Built at Doncaster Works and introduced to service on 23 October 1942 as 3843, it would be renumbered as 3973 in 1946, before eventually becoming 63973. Its final home would be 36E Retford (GC) where it would be withdrawn on 22 September 1963 and be cut up by Rigleys, Bulwell Forest in 1964. (*H. K. Boulter/Author's collection*)

ROD Class 04/1 63577 reposes on shed, in this undated shot. Originally built at Gorton in December 1911 as GCR Class 8K No. 26, the LNER numbered it 5026, then it would become 3577 in 1946 and BR 63577. Withdrawn from Langwith in December 1963, it would be disposed of at Doncaster Works in February 1964. (*Author's collection*)

C12 4-4-2T	7351/55/57/84
N5 0-6-2T	9284/319/23/27
Q1 0-8-0	9928/29

In March 1949, the provisional shed codes for the Western Section of the Eastern Region were announced, giving Langwith Junction a code of 46E. However, in October 1949 the separate sections of the Eastern Region merged and the codes were reissued. This time, Langwith would be given the code of 40E, as a sub-shed of the Lincoln District. This situation lasted until 1 February 1958, when a major transfer of lines and depots from one region to another took place. Some former GCR depots and lines were absorbed into the London Midland Region, and simultaneously there was a reorganization of the Eastern Region, which resulted in the abolition of the Colwick and Peterborough Districts and the expansion of the Sheffield District. Langwith now came under the Sheffield umbrella and therefore gained its final code of 41J. The mid-1950s saw an increasing number of WD 2-8-0s working alongside the 04s.

In the mid-1950s, a much larger dual roundhouse type was proposed by BR. This new depot would have been supplied with the most modern facilities for steam:

Overhead sand hoppers
Kelbus Sand Plant
Water softener plant
Overhead water supply to all turntable roads
Two 70-foot turntables
A turn round pit
A 200-ton coaling plant
Repair shop
Wheel lathe
Wheel drop
Ash wagon road
200-foot wet ash pits
Ambulance room
Stores
Machine shop
Boiler shop
Tool and oil store

Unfortunately, again, nothing came of the proposals.

The First Diesels Arrive

The first diesels to arrive at Langwith Junction were 350-hp 0-6-0 shunters of later classes 08 and 10, to take over the local shunting duties from steam. These were

A visitor to the shed in the form of North-British-built K1 Mogul 2-6-0 62054 on 15 June 1958. Introduced in November 1949, this loco would end its days allocated to 36E Retford (GC) on 31 December 1964, before being disposed of in the North East at Hughes Bolckow in North Blyth in 1965. (*H. B. P. Priestley/Author's collection*)

Class 04/7 63634 at Langwith. This was one of the forty-one of the type that were rebuilt in 1939 with shortened oxygen boilers and fireboxes but retaining the original cab. It stands in front of the sheer legs that used to lift locos to allow wheels to be replaced. (*Lawson Little*)

WD J94 0-6-0ST 68080 is on loan to Hucknall Colliery from Langwith 23 April 1960. It seems to be fitted with some sort of water treatment device on the tank front; maybe the water at Hucknall was particularly hard. The J94 0-6-0s arrived at Langwith to replace the N5s on local trip work, but they were soon superseded by diesel shunters. (*A. Swain/Author's collection*)

Along with two unidentified sisters, WD 2-8-0 90551 is seen at Langwith. By this time, the class were heavily run down and not much longer for this world; this one's last shed would be 36A Doncaster, from where it was withdrawn on 30 April 1966 and disposed of at Drapers of Hull in October 1966. (*Author's collection*)

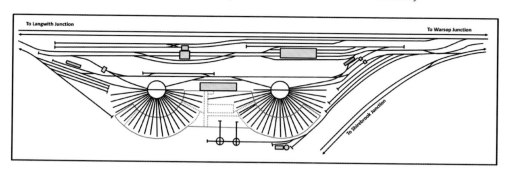

A plan of the proposed new steam depot at Langwith Junction, dated 1954–55. This was originally drawn by Bob Johnston, with information supplied by Lawson Little, but has been redrawn for clarity. (*Author's collection*)

D3325, D3701, and D4053/57/60/61/66/67/69/85. The first mainline diesel to be worked by the men at Langwith was D5567, which was given trials on colliery pilot and trip workings during the first week of February 1960. Based at Darnall, driven by Darnall men, but piloted by Langwith crews, the workings were:

1 February 1960 Welbeck pilot
2nd Warsop–Mottram
3rd Rufford Colliery pilot
4th Bilsthorpe Colliery
5th Mansfield Colliery Sidings to Immingham.

By 1961, the last Class N5 had departed, being replaced by former War Department (WD) J94 0-6-0ST, then Langwith received a batch of 9F 2-10-0s, which did not reign long as their long wheelbase did not fare well on some of the colliery tracks. The steam depot was to have been converted to a diesel depot by September 1962 but progress was delayed, and by November 1962 there were still approximately forty steam locos in use.

The men at Langwith were sent for further training on Brush Type 2 (Class 31) diesel locomotives at Darnall Depot, because there were plans made during 1962 for Langwith to become the operating base of twelve Brush Type 2 diesel locomotives. These were to be engaged in one of the pioneer Eastern Region Class 7* freight workings, covering coal hauls from Mansfield Concentration Sidings and Warsop to Immingham, Whitemoor (March) and New England (Peterborough). These were 41A Darnall allocated locomotives out-based at Langwith, but still maintained at Darnall. One locomotive was changed daily on a working to the Rotherwood exchange sidings. They were booked to work about ten return trips a day on what the drivers knew as an 'out and home' basis, and crew changes would normally be undertaken at either Pyewipe Junction, near Lincoln, or on the Bardney Branch just the other side of Lincoln. The Brush Type 2s were initially serviced in the old carriage shed at Langwith Junction, while fuelling was accomplished from rail tankers which were pressurised with air to force the fuel out and into the locomotives' fuel tanks.

The sign of things to come as Brush Type 2 D5538 sits with Robinson 04 2-8-0 63706 in the carriage shed in this image, which is dated 1 November 1965. The 04 had arrived at Langwith on 13 June 1965 and withdrawn from there on 26 September 1965, so by the time of the photo it was already withdrawn. As for the Brush, this was a 41A Tinsley engine at the time: it became 31190 on 1 January 1973 and would be withdrawn on 27 September 1991, meeting its end at C. F. Booth's scrapyard in Rotherham during June 1994. (*K. C. H. Fairey/Derek Talbot collection*)

In June 1965, the Class 9F 2-10-0s took over many of the remaining duties of the steam shed. This enabled most of the class 04 2-8-0s and WD 2-8-0s to be stood down, however 13 June 1965 saw 04s 63691/7 63732/9, 63843/50 still in use. The final Belpair boiler example to remain in service, 63902, was at this time stored awaiting withdrawal, on the same date, the only diesel on shed was Clayton D8608 (later Class 17).

By 19 June 1965, the following steam locomotives were allocated to 41J:

4MT 2-6-0	43064
B1 4-6-0	61313/5//72/94
04 2-8-0	63589/90/3612/30/46/50/79/91/97, 63701/6/32/39/68
	63828/43/50/68/93
WD 2-8-0	90043/69/88/148/153/271/75/92/301/98/401/18/49/558/658/719
9F 2-10-0	92039/40/41/42/141/44/45/46/48/49/73/78/79/82/86/89/91/2200

Scheduled for closure in October 1965, there was a temporary reprieve, as some of the replacement diesels were late on delivery. The few remaining steam duties were covered by a dwindling band of grimy WD 2-8-0s, but by the end of January 1966 just three (90153/572/719) remained serviceable. Finally, on 6 February 1966, the last fires were dropped, and Langwith closed to steam after seventy years. The last steam

locomotives were assembled in the old carriage shed to await scrap. These were WD 2-8-0s 90043/69/149/153/418/449/572/719, with the last two 04s (63612 and 63843) having left for Cox & Danks at Wadsley Bridge on 7 January 1966.

Following closure, the brick engine shed was purchased by W. H. Davis Wagon Works and rebuilt as a workshop, and this still survives. The Mitchell Coaling Plant was eventually demolished and the carriage shed, turntable and a collection of vintage carriage bodies were swept away along with much of the track.

The site still sees rail activity today, as W. H. Davis has won several contracts for the construction and conversion of wagons, which will see them busy for some time to come.

Opposite above: In the last full year of operation, a grimy 9F 2-10-0 92144 is seen with equally grimy 2-8-0 classes 04 and WD at Langwith on 30 August 1965. The 9F 2-10-0 had a criminally short life, being introduced to service on 31 August 1957 and withdrawn, far from life expired, from 38A Colwick on 31 December 1965. It would be disposed of at T. W. Ward's yard in Beighton in April 1966, still less than ten years old. (*Author's collection*)

Opposite below: An aerial view of the W. H. Davis Wagon Works and the former Langwith Junction depot. The former Leen Valley Line curves round towards the road bridge at the bottom of the photo, this now being truncated just before the bridge. A grey-roofed van sits on the remains of the former Down Line of the Branch. To the right of the stack of red containers, beneath the yellow crane, is the remains of the depot. The Nottingham to Worksop line runs in the limestone cutting to the top right of the photo. (*Courtesy W. H. Davis Ltd*)

5

Signalling

The LD&ECR was provided with comprehensive signalling from the outset, the Sykes Lock and Block system of working being introduced along the railway. Invented by W. R. Sykes in 1874 and patented in 1875, this system was adopted by a number of railway companies, as at that time it was far ahead of other systems in terms of safety interlocking. It ensured that signals were interlocked with both block indications and train movements, long before the development of track circuits. The system was found on the Great Eastern, North British and most of the constituent companies of the Southern Railway; the idea was to ensure that a signalman could not allow a train to pass into the next section until the previous one was proved by the equipment to have passed through that section.

A typical two-position instrument combined a semaphore block indicator, an upper tablet showing received signals, and a lower tablet showing signals sent. The instrument had a plunger, which was pressed in to send an electrical signal to another signal box, and the switch hook, which pivoted over to mechanically prevent the plunger being pressed. This instrument is used in connection with the usual bells.

The usual method of working was: to offer a train, signalman 'A' used his block bell to send the required bell signal to signalman 'B'. If signalman 'B' could accept the train, he pressed the plunger, which sent an electrical signal to unlock the other signalman's instrument, so that his upper tablet then showed 'Free', and allowed him to pull his lever and pull his signal to 'Off'. When 'A' sent 'train entering section' (two beats on the bell) to 'B', then 'B' moved the switch hook over onto the plunger, which changed the block indicator to 'train on' and also physically prevented him pressing the plunger again. The lower tablet of the intial signalman's instrument then showed 'train on' (the LD&ECR instruments did not have this 'train on' feature; the hook switch being turned was regarded as an equivalent). 'A' then permitted the train to proceed, after which he replaced his signal to 'Danger' with the upper tablet stating 'Locked'. When the train passed 'B' and released a treadle, the signal there could be replaced to 'Danger' and the switch hook moved off of the plunger. This changed the lower tablet to blank at 'A' and 'B'. 'B' could then accept a following train from 'A'. If a train had been accepted but could not proceed, a key was rotated in the 'Emergency Release' keyhole, which would restore the instrument to normal. The use of the key was to be noted in the Train Register Book.

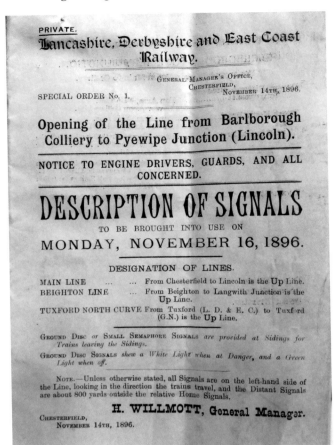

Held in the National Railway Museum collection is a circular dated 14 November 1896, which was issued to all concerned when the line between Barlborough Colliery Junction and Pyewipe Junction was ready for opening on Monday 16 November 1896. (*Author*)

Between Chesterfield and Tuxford, the signalling was contracted to Saxby and Farmer (S&F), with signal boxes being built to a design unique to the LD&ECR, while Tuxford to Pyewipe Sidings and the Beighton Branch were contracted to the Railway Signal Co. (RSCo.). All the signal boxes were similar in outline: the S&F boxes had three panes deep operating floor windows, decorative bargeboards and gable window/vents two panes across, whereas the RSCo.-built boxes had four panes deep operating floor windows, plain bargeboards and gable window/vents four panes across, the design being reminiscent of the GNR. After takeover of the company in 1907, GCR Type 5 boxes were built along the routes. The signals were originally GNR style somersault type, however they differed slightly, in that the lamp was in line with the arms, and those on goods lines had ringed arms. Ground signals were revolving discs showing a white light for danger and green for all clear, with the signal number painted in black on the white face of the disc.

A circular dated 14 November 1896 was issued to all concerned when the line between Barlborough Colliery Junction and Pyewipe Junction was ready for opening on Monday 16 November 1896. It describes the signals to be found at each signal box then open, and a summary of it is laid out here approximating its style:

Barlborough Colliery Junction

For Trains to Lincoln
    Up Distant..........................In use for contractors' trains only.
    Up Home (on Down side).......In use for contractors' trains only.
    Up Starting for trains from
        Colliery...................Between colliery line and run round siding.

For Trains from Lincoln
    Facing points from Down Main to Colliery
    Down Distant Bracket
        (On upside)............... Top Arm, Main Line.
      Lower Arm, Colliery Line.
    Down home bracket...........Top Arm, Main Line.
      Lower arm, Colliery line.
    Signals in Colliery...............Stop Signal, at Colliery End on the
      'Run Round' Sidings for trains for
      Empty Sidings.
      Stop Signal in the fork between 'Run
      Round' Sidings and colliery line for
      trains leaving Full Sidings for 'Run
      Round' sidings.
    Down Starting.....................(In use for contractors' trains only.)

It went on to describe the route through to Lincoln with signal boxes at Clowne; Creswell station (signals not yet in use); Creswell Colliery Junction; Norwood Level Crossing (controlled by a gatehouse keeper); Langwith Colliery Junction; and Langwith Junction station, which was the largest box on the line and contained a Saxby and Farmer sixty-six-lever frame when built.

Langwith Junction Station

For Trains to Lincoln
    Up Distant Bracket.............Left Arm, Main Line.
      Right Arm not in use.
    Up Home Bracket...............Left Arm, Main Line.
      Right Arm not in use.
    Up Starting Bracket...........Left Arm, Main Line.
      Right Arm not in use.
    Up Advance Starting...........300 yards ahead of signal box.
On the Beighton Line.
    Up Distant Bracket.............Left Arm, Main Line.
      Right Arm not in use.

Above left: Signalling along the Beighton Branch was contracted to the Railway Signal Company, and one of their boxes was Langwith Colliery Junction, an all-wood style box. Notice the asymmetric roof line to accommodate the signalman's 'privy'. This view is from August 1969; the box closed in June 1971. (*Adrian Stretton*)

Above right: Langwith Junction signal box was the largest box on the LD&ECR, and opened with the line from Barlborough Colliery Junction to Pyewipe Junction. A report dated 28 December 1896 stated that it had a Saxby and Farmer sixty-four-lever frame that included nine spare levers. When the route from Langwith to Chesterfield opened, a second report dated 7 October 1897 showed that there were now sixty-six levers and five spares. On the opening of the GNR Leen Valley Line, a report dated 7 October 1901 showed that the frame had been extended to eighty-one levers, of which five were spares. Finally, on 20 December 1902, a disc signal was removed and replaced by two semaphores, this making the frame seventy-seven worked and four spares. The next change came with the opening of the curve to Shirebrook Junction on the Midland Railway. Another report, dated 10 July 1905, showed that a new signal box at Langwith East Junction was opened: this had the effect of more new signals being controlled from Langwith Junction, and the frame became eighty-one worked levers with no spares. With the closure of Langwith East Junction on 28 April 1929, its operations were absorbed by Langwith Junction box, so the frame was again extended to eighty-five levers, with the new levers being placed to the left of No. 1 lever and lettered 'A' to 'D'.

To accommodate the new levers, a small extension to the building had to be made, which was visible by the use of slightly narrower windows at the west end. The new levers controlled motor points that were installed on the former Langwith Junction East Nos 24 and 25 for access to Warsop Loops. The box closed on 10 November 1974, becoming redundant with the construction of the new curve from the Midland Railway route towards Warsop, and the removal of Bridge 37 over the Midland line. (*Derek Talbot*)

Up Home Bracket (on down side) Left Arm, Main Line.
    Right Arm not in use.
Up Starting Bracket............Left Arm, Main Line.
    Right Arm not in use.

For Trains from Lincoln
    Down Distant Bracket.........Left Arm, Main Line.
        Right Arm, Beighton line.
    Down Home Bracket...........Left Arm, Main Line.
        Right Arm, Beighton line.
    Down Starting.....................Main Line, fixed at the end of the Down platform.
    Down Advanced Starting...Main line 200 yards ahead of Starting signal.
    Down Starting.....................Beighton Line, fixed at the end of the Down Branch
    Platform.
    Down Advanced Starting...Beighton Line, Arm fixed below bracket on the Up Home
    post.

The lever frame here was extended to eighty-five levers in 1930. Continuing on came Warsop Junction, Warsop Main Colliery Line (signals not yet in use), Warsop station, and Clipstone Goods Siding. The latter was described as connected on the Up line only, with no fixed signals, but worked by an electrical arrangement between Warsop and Edwinstowe signal boxes, it was in effect a Ground Frame.

After Edwinstowe came Ollerton, Boughton, Boughton Level Crossing (situated one mile Tuxford-side of the station and controlled by a gatehouse keeper), Tuxford station, and Tuxford West Junction.

Tuxford West Junction

For Trains to Lincoln
    Note—The running lines between Tuxford West Junction (LD&ECR) and Tuxford
    Junction (GNR) are termed the North Curve.
    Facing points to North Curve leading to GNR from Main Line.

    Up Distant...........................Main line. Right-hand lower arm on
        Tuxford Station up advanced starting post
    Up Distant...........................North Curve, Left Arm on Tuxford station
        up advanced starting post
    Up Home Bracket................Right Arm, Main Line
        Left Arm, North Curve
    Up Starting..........................Main line. On right-hand side 315 yards ahead of
    signal box
    Up Starting.........................For North Curve

Above left: One of the smallest boxes along the line was Tuxford Central, a Saxby and Farmer box, which will feature in Volume Two. Opened in 1896, this had a twenty-two-lever frame and worked to Boughton Station and Tuxford West. It closed on 25 March 1984. (*Adrian Stretton*)

Above right: Signalman Mick Bennett at work in Tuxford Central box, showing part of the twenty-two-lever frame. (*Adrian Stretton*)

For Trains from Lincoln

    Down Distant......Lower Arm on Tuxford Junction Passenger Station Down
                    Starting post (700 yards from Signal Box)
    Down Distant......From North Curve. Arm fixed on GN Junction Down Starting post
    Down Home...... Fixed on Up side of curve, between shunting spur and Main Line

Next came Tuxford Junction passenger station (signals not yet in use), Fledborough, Clifton-on-Trent, Thorney Level Crossing (situated about a mile Lincoln-side of Clifton-on-Trent Station and controlled by a gatehouse keeper), Doddington and Harby, Doddington Siding (not yet open for traffic), Contractors Ballast Siding (laid about 1 mile Doddington and Harby side of Skellingthorpe station and worked by Annett's Key, which was kept in Skellingthorpe signal box), Skellingthorpe, and finally Pyewipe West, after which came the GNR box at Pyewipe Junction.

The Sykes Lock and Block system suffered with a design defect in that it had to have a release mechanism, the previously mentioned emergency release key. It was very easy for the signalman to assume that the equipment had failed when, in actual fact, it was preventing a signal being cleared because a train was still in section. Over a period of time, the system would be superseded along the LD&ECR by standard GCR block instruments, some of which remained until closure of the signal boxes.

6

Removal of Bridge No. 37

The LD&ECR crossed the MR Worksop to Mansfield line at Shirebrook North by steel girder Bridge No. 37 and, in 1904, connections were made with flying junctions down to the MR known as 'The New Foundout'. There is more on these junctions in Volume Two. By early 1974, Bridge No. 37 had come up for renewal: a document issued for a special train in August 1974 showed that the bridge was in such a condition that the train was banned from crossing it while loaded. Rather than renew the bridge, it was decided to construct a short chord from the LD&ECR at Bridge No. 37A on a falling gradient of 1-in-100 down to the MR Worksop-Mansfield line, at the site of the closed LMS Welbeck colliery branch cutting, and dispense with Bridge No. 37 completely.

The original plans for the chord showed that it was to be double-track, and it also showed that the line from Langwith Junction via the remains of the Beighton Branch to Norwood was to be singled. The hypothesis is that the original idea included retaining access to W. H. Davis by utilising the line from Norwood to Langwith Junction. Of course, the later reinstatement of the Down side 'New Foundout' to give access to the W. H. Davis works did away with this requirement and saved a lot of track work. The construction of the curve as a single track instead of double would also have had a cost cutting benefit. The new chord would also allow the section of line through Shirebrook North Station, via the Beighton Branch and the connection to Norwood, to be dispensed with giving more savings.

The construction of this chord entailed huge works to blast a route through the limestone cutting of the MR. These works were documented in photographs by a local BR S&T employee, Derek Talbot.

The works also involved a lot of train movements. A document dated 8 August 1974 was distributed to all concerned by C. W. Rawcliffe, Sheffield's Divisional Civil Engineer, although the document shows work beginning from Monday 15 July. It shows all the planned movements to be made in connection with the work and, on another page, it stated that 'the crane used would be the 12-ton diesel crane, which could be stabled at Shirebrook MPD overnight thus alleviating the needs to provide protection'. Scrawled on the back of the document was the loco number 08263 and the train headcode G14. The new chord came into use on 11 November 1974, and all remaining sections of the LD&ECR to the west of Shirebrook were dispensed with.

Bridge No. 37 looking east towards Bridge No. 37A and Warsop Junction before work began. (*Derek Talbot*)

Looking towards Bridge No. 37A, rock drilling is underway. (*Derek Talbot*)

Viewed south from the cutting of the Midland line as work starts to cut away the cutting side. The track has been slewed to allow the machinery to cut away the limestone sides. (*Derek Talbot*)

Viewed from track level, looking north. The former LMS Welbeck Colliery Branch cutting is on the extreme right. The signals are Shirebrook Junction No. 33 Outer Home, with Shirebrook Station 'A' distant signal beneath. (*Derek Talbot*)

The rock face has been cut back and the new trackbed is being made. The nearest dumper truck is heading towards the Welbeck Colliery Branch cutting, where its load of limestone will be dumped. (*Derek Talbot*)

Ballast has now been laid and the pointwork is in position. The Up Main part of the crossover points (which would become No. 27A) and the lead onto the single line (No. 26) were installed on 2 June 1974, while the Down Main end of the crossover road (No. 27B) was laid on 7 July 1974. All were worked from Shirebrook Junction signal box. The former LMS Welbeck Colliery branch opposite the signal is now almost infilled. (*Derek Talbot*)

As viewed from Bridge No. 37A looking towards Langwith Junction, the long footbridge across the former station can be seen. The new cutting to the right of the main line awaits track laying. (*Derek Talbot*)

Track now laid, the chord awaits connection and full commissioning at the east end. (*Derek Talbot*)

The mess left behind after removal of Bridge No. 37 in May 1975, with the chord on the right in full operation. Langwith Junction No. 7 signal post lies at a drunken angle waiting to be removed and cable troughs are stacked up for reuse elsewhere. A rake of refurbished 16-ton wagons are in W. H. Davis's yard, and the now-closed Langwith Junction signal box can be seen in front of the long footbridge. (*John S. Gilks*)

Once the work to build the chord was completed, Bridge No. 37 was dismantled and that saw the end of trains through Shirebrook North. However, as W. H. Davis still required access to their wagon works, a new connection was made from the MR by relaying the former Down Shirebrook Junction to Shirebrook North connection, part of the 'New Foundout' that can be seen curving off right. (*Derek Talbot*)

This document is now part of the Neil Baker collection and is transcribed here.

Shirebrook-Installation of new curve, Ballast Train Workings

Monday 15 July engine Class 08, ex Shirebrook MPD 07.30 to Warsop Up Sidings, work as instructed with 10-ton crane, manned to 16.30, engine Class 47, ex-Shirebrook MPD 15.00 to Warsop Up Sidings, attach to material train and return to Beighton Depot, detach wagons where instructed and return LE to MPD manned to 22.00

Tuesday, Wednesday, Thursday, Friday, 16, 17, 18, 19 July, engine Class 08 ex-Shirebrook MPD 07.30 to Warsop Up Sidings, work as instructed with 10-ton crane, manned to 16.30. Sunday 21 July, ballast engine and crane working arrangement by P. Way Supervisor (Shirebrook) crane to be returned to Warsop Up Sidings.

Monday, Tuesday, Wednesday 22, 23, 24 July, engine Class 08 ex-Shirebrook MPD 07.30 to Warsop Up Sidings, work as instructed with 10-ton crane, manned to 16.30.

Wednesday 24 July, engine Class 31, ex-Shirebrook MPD, 06.30 to Beighton Depot, attach to 8 loaded slag hoppers and draw to Warsop Up Sidings. On completion return to Beighton Depot, place wagons in sidings and return LE to depot, manned to 20.00. Note: Crane to be returned to Beighton Depot.

Monday 29 July engine Class 31 ex Shirebrook MPD, 06.00 to Beighton Depot, attach to 10-ton crane and 2 × 'Arneke' wagons (provisional) draw to Warsop Up Sidings, detach wagons, engine returns LE to depot. Engine Class 08, ex-Shirebrook MPD 09.00 to Warsop Up Sidings work as instructed, manned to 16.30. Tuesday and Wednesday 30 and 31 July, engine Class 08, ex Shirebrook MPD to Warsop Up Sidings, manned to 16.30.

Thursday 1 August (provisional item) engine Class 31, ex-Shirebrook MPD 07.00 to Warsop Up Sidings, work as instructed, on completion return 10-ton crane and 2 × 'Arneke' wagons to Beighton Depot, manned to 20.00.

Wednesday 7 August engine Class 31, ex Shirebrook MPD 06.00 to Beighton Depot, attach to 12 loaded slag hoppers and draw to Warsop Up Sidings, work as instructed on completion return to Beighton Depot, place wagons in sidings, engine detach and return LE to Depot, manned to 20.00.

Tuesday 13 August, engine Class 31, ex Shirebrook MPD 06.00 to Beighton Depot, attach to 12 loaded slag hoppers and 2 × 'Arneke' wagons, draw to Warsop Up Sidings, work as instructed, manned to 17.00.

Wednesday 14 August, engine Class 31, ex-Shirebrook MPD 07.30 to Warsop Up Sidings, work as instructed, on completion return wagons to Beighton Depot, engine detach and return LE to Depot.

Sunday 18 August, ballast train and crane working to be arranged by P. Way Supervisor. Sunday 1 September, ballast train and crane workings to be detailed on special circular

Monday 2 September Note: Crane to be stabled at Warsop Up Sidings or Shirebrook MPD on Sunday 1st September, engine Class 08 ex-Shirebrook MPD 07.30 to Warsop Up Sidings, work as instructed manned to 16.00

Once the works were completed, Bridge No. 37 was removed for scrap, and today there is no sign that it had ever been there. This concludes Volume One; in Volume Two, we will continue the journey towards Lincoln.